CULTURES OF THE WORLD

AUSTRALIA

Vijeya & Sundran Rajendra

MARSHALL CAVENDISH
New York • London • Sydney

Reference edition published 1994 by
Marshall Cavendish Corporation
2415 Jerusalem Avenue
P.O. Box 587
North Bellmore
New York 11710

© Times Editions Pte Ltd 1994, 1991

Originated and designed by
Times Books International, an imprint of
Times Editions Pte Ltd

Printed in Singapore

Library of Congress Cataloging-in-Publication Data:
Rajendra, Vijeya, 1936–
    Australia / Vijeya Rajendra and Sundran
    Rajendra.—Reference ed.
      p. cm.—(Cultures Of The World)
    Includes bibliographical references and index.
    Summary: Australia's emergence as an important multicultural society in the twentieth century is examined in context with the unique geography and history of this island continent.
    ISBN 1-85435-400-0
    1. Australia—Juvenile literature [1. Australia.]
I. Rajendra, Sundran, 1967–. II. Title. III Series.
DU96.R34 1991
994—dc20   91–15864
          CIP
           AC

Cultures of the World

Editorial Director	Shirley Hew
Managing Editor	Shova Loh
Editors	Falak Kagda
	Michael Spilling
	Sue Sismondo
	Roslind Varghese
	Azra Moiz
	Elizabeth Koh Kanematsu
	Jon Burbank
	Jim Goodman
Picture Editor	Yee May Kaung
Production	Edmund Lam
Design	Tuck Loong
	Ronn Yeo
	Felicia Wong
	Loo Chuan Ming
Illustrators	Kelvin Sim
	Cherine Lim
	Andrew Chan
	Anuar bin Abdul Rahim
MCC Editorial Director	Evelyn M. Fazio

INTRODUCTION

AUSTRALIA is the land "down under." Behind the image of kangaroos and cuddly koalas lies a vast continent of mystery and contradiction. From tropical rainforests to endless deserts, from golden beaches to ancient mountains, it is a land of flood and drought, heat and cold, fire and water.

The 17.5 million inhabitants of the continent of Australia live in one of the most cosmopolitan, highly urbanized states in the world. Today this young nation, built upon the heritage of the West, is preparing to take a greater role among its neighbors in the East.

As part of the series *Cultures of the World*, this book is an introduction to Australia and its people, their lifestyle, language, and customs.

Australians are friendly and informal, and they are very fond of their animal emblem, the kangaroo.

CONTENTS

Bush roads are dotted with signs showing Australia's unique animals.

CONTENTS

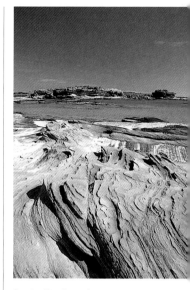

Australia has been called the "Oldest Continent" because much of it's rock was formed in the Pre-cambrian Age, that is, 5 billion years ago.

GEOGRAPHY

AUSTRALIA, the sixth largest country in the world, lies in the Southern Hemisphere, between 11° and 44° south latitude and 113° and 154° east longitude. A nation of few people and vast lands, its population of 17.5 million inhabits an area of land about the same size as the continental United States, or about one and a half times the size of Europe. Mainland Australia, with an area of 2,967,909 square miles, is so enormous that it is regarded as the world's seventh and smallest continent.

The country is divided into six states: Queensland, New South Wales, Victoria, Tasmania, South Australia, and Western Australia. In addition, it has three internal territories (Northern Territory, Australian Capital Territory, and Jervis Bay Territory) and seven external territories (Christmas Island, Cocos Islands, Norfolk Island, Coral Sea Islands, Ashmore and Cartier Islands, Heard Island, McDonald Islands, and Australian Antarctic Territory).

Left: **In contrast to the central deserts, the coast offers a picture of lush vegetation.**

Opposite: **Everything in Australia is on a large scale. Four deserts, covering about 800,000 square miles of wasteland, make up the country's hot, dry "Red Center."**

The Great Sandy Desert in the northwest of the country stretches as far as the eye can see.

A LAND AS OLD AS TIME

The continent of Australia is often described as an "old land" because the geological activity that created the country's mountains, rivers, and plains ceased millions of years ago. Earthquakes are rare in Australia and the last volcanic eruption occurred more than 5,000 years ago. Over the centuries, wind and water have eroded the land's more spectacular features, leaving vast stretches of flat, featureless plains. The highest mountain in Australia, Mount Kosciusko, is only 7,310 feet above sea level.

Mount Kosciusko lies in the southern part of the Eastern Highlands, a belt of elevated land stretching down the length of Australia's east coast from northern Queensland to central Victoria—a distance of 1,860 miles. Settlers first arriving in Australia called these highlands the Great Dividing Range since they were an obstacle blocking their exploration of the lands farther to the west.

Beyond the Great Dividing Range lie the great plains of the Central Lowlands. They are remarkable for what lies underneath them—vast underground stores of water trapped in porous sandstone between beds of hard rock. Farmers use windmills to pump this water (called artesian water) to the surface to irrigate crops and feed livestock.

The western two-thirds of the Australian continent is an arid, flat surface called the Great Western Plateau. This ancient region, rich in minerals such as iron ore, bauxite, and uranium, includes many deserts. One such desert is the 434 mile-wide Nullarbor Plain. Although it sounds like a native Aboriginal name, Nullarbor is actually a Latin phrase meaning "no tree," in reference to its treeless landscape. Travelers can cross the plain on the Trans-Australian railway, which possesses the longest straight stretch of railway in the world—297 miles.

Windmills pump artesian water to ground level. The water is then stored in reservoirs and used for irrigation and feeding livestock.

THE GREAT BARRIER REEF

The Great Barrier Reef is an 82,800 square mile-complex of islands and coral reefs stretching over 1,196 miles along Australia's northeast coast. Built by countless numbers of tiny coral polyps over 2 million years, it is the largest structure ever created by any animal.

Today, the reef is one of the world's greatest tourist attractions. Visitors look at the coral through glass-bottom boats, and swimmers and divers get a first hand view of the amazing variety of creatures that inhabit the reef. There are giant clams, so big that their shells can be used as bath tubs. Colorful anemone fish rest among the deadly tentacles of anemones. At night, ghost crabs scuttle upon the reef's beaches in search of insects and other small animals.

The Great Barrier Reef has been declared a national park to protect the coral and the reef's wildlife from human exploitation. However, thousands of square miles of reef have been destroyed in recent years. The culprit is the crown-of-thorns starfish, which feeds on the polyps that form the reef, leaving behind large areas of dead, colorless coral that is soon swept away by the sea. In spite of attempts to destroy them, the starfish population has increased dramatically over the past few years.

CLIMATE

Because it spans both the tropical and temperate regions of the Southern Hemisphere, Australia experiences a variety of climates. The continent's immense interior gives way to hot, wet monsoonal tropical regions in the north. Bordering the desert is a dry region of semi-desert that acts as a transition to the more humid regions of the north, east, and south. The southeast coast, where most of Australia's population lives, is cooler and drier. The southwest is very hot and dry in summer, but milder and wetter in winter. The climate can be likened to that of the Mediterranean countries of Europe, or to California.

In general, summers in Australia are hot to very hot. Dry winds blowing from a westerly direction send temperatures in the country's interior soaring to over 104°F during the months of December to February (summer in the Southern Hemisphere). Coastal regions are cooler, due to offshore breezes. Because of the heat and lack of rain, bushfires rage through the tinder-dry landscape, destroying half a million acres of forest and grassland every year.

In the south of the country, temperatures drop considerably in winter and frosts are common. During the winter months of June, July, and August, snow falls in the Eastern Highlands of Victoria and New South Wales. The highlands boast a number of skiing resorts.

Bushfires, fanned by the dry winds, burn up vast areas of forest and grassland.

More than 1,000 different types of plants grow in the Arnhem Land Plateau, on the northern tip of the Northern Territory.

The hot temperatures of the inland coupled with the lack of rain mean that 70% of Australia receives less than 20 inches of rain a year, making it the world's driest continent. Farming in these areas is difficult, but not impossible, thanks to the exploitation of artesian water and the construction of many irrigation schemes. In contrast, the east, the southwest tip, and the tropical regions in the north are considerably wetter. Cairns, a town on the northern coast of Queensland, regularly receives more than 100 inches of rain a year.

In most areas of Australia, there are wide changes in rainfall from year to year. Droughts in inland areas are common and may last for several years. All Australians are affected by the long and widespread droughts since the country's wealth depends to a large extent on farming.

NATIVE ANIMALS

When the first Europeans arrived in Australia and started to explore the country, they could hardly believe the strange animals they saw. They, and the settlers who came after them, were especially fascinated by the various species of marsupials that they met in Australia. Marsupials are mammals that raise their offspring in a pouch on their body until the latter are a reasonable size and can fend for themselves. They have adapted very well to the harsh

Australian environment. The marsupial family includes possums that glide from tree to tree, koalas, kangaroos, wombats, and carnivores such as the fierce Tasmanian Devil.

Kangaroos, a common sight in the Australian bush (countryside), look like enormous mice standing on their hind legs. Like other marsupials, female kangaroos carry their offspring (called joeys) in a pouch located in front of their abdomen. Kangaroos move by hopping on their powerful rear legs. They can travel as far as 30 feet in a single jump. When fighting, kangaroos lash out with their hind legs or punch with their smaller front paws. One kangaroo that escaped from a zoo in Adelaide knocked out a policeman with one punch before it was recaptured.

Many marsupials are found in Australia. The kangaroo (*above*) is the country's animal emblem, while the Tasmanian Devil (*below*) has acquired a fierce reputation.

Unlike the kangaroo, which feeds on grass, the koala only eats the leaves of the eucalyptus. Koalas spend most of their lives clinging to tree branches. When they are old enough to leave the pouch, young koalas catch a ride on their mother's back. Koalas appear to be shy, cuddly creatures, but many a bushman knows how sharp their claws are when they are cornered!

The most unusual creature of the bush is the duck-billed platypus. The animal literally defied description for those who first saw it. Although the platypus' body is covered with fur like that of other mammals, it has a duck-like bill and webbed feet like birds. It lays eggs deep in its underwater burrow. Another remarkable animal is the mallee-fowl, which has invented a form of reverse cycle air-conditioning for its nest. The female bird covers its eggs under a mound of dirt. It keeps the eggs at a constant temperature by adding or removing dirt from the mound.

OLD TOM

Inside the museum in Eden, a fishing town in Victoria, is the skeleton of "Old Tom," a killer whale that formed an extraordinary partnership with the local fishermen. These fishermen hunted whalebone whales, which migrated along Australia's east coast during winter.

Whenever a whale strayed close to Eden, Old Tom and his pack herded it into the town's bay. If no fishermen were about, some of the pack went to the shore and raised a terrific noise. The fishermen quickly recognized the signal to rush to their boats. While the sailors were hurrying out, the killers attacked the unfortunate whale. By the time the fishermen arrived, the whale was battered and exhausted, and was easily killed. In return for their help, the fishermen allowed the killer pack to drag the dead whale to the sea bottom where they feasted on the tongue and lips. A day later the sailors returned to tow the rest of the body to shore.

This bizarre partnership lasted nearly 90 years. But, after World War I, the killers started to disappear. They were killed at sea by Norwegian sailors fishing off the coast. Once the killer whales were gone, the whalebone whales stopped coming into Eden. The town's whaling industry closed down. In 1930 Old Tom, well over 90 years old now, made his last visit to Eden. The next day he was found dead, drifting in the bay. Local sailors, who recognized their old friend, dragged his body to shore. The skeleton was sent to the town's museum where to this day it remains on display.

The emu is a flightless bird, the second largest in the world after the ostrich.

The duck-billed platypus combines the characteristics of both mammals and birds.

Opposite page: **Contrary to popular belief, the koala is not a bear, but a marsupial, which feeds exclusively on the leaves of the eucalyptus tree.**

The largest bird in Australia is the emu. Like the ostrich, it will eat just about anything. One story tells how a flock of emus devoured a farmer's new steel plough. He was crestfallen until one of his workers killed the unfortunate emus, removed the steel pieces from their stomachs and rebuilt the plough!

Australia has several highly dangerous native animals. The venom of the tiger snake of southern Australia is so deadly that one drop can kill a person. The tiny red-back spider is also highly toxic. One of its favorite homes is under the toilet seat in bathrooms in the bush. Crocodiles and sharks, like the great white pointer, have claimed more than 400 swimmers.

The baobab is quite common in Australia, where it is also called the bottle tree.

NATIVE PLANTS

In Australia's wetter regions, native trees (eucalyptuses) appear in open woodlands similar to the savanna of Africa. Farther toward the coast, dense forests grow. In the north, there are monsoon forests, similar to the forests of Indonesia and Malaysia. Rainforests and eucalyptus woodlands line the southern coast and Eastern Highlands. Although these forests cover only a fraction of Australia's land, they are very important. Rainforests contain many types of trees that are cut down for timber. Ironbarks, red gums, and other species of eucalyptus are also used by the timber industry.

In the dry interior where rain is scarce, large plains of hard and woody clumps of grass (spinifex) stretch as far as the eye can see. Farther south, there are forests of bushes up to 26 feet tall, called "scrub." Many of these plants are able to store large amounts of water or extract moisture from deep below the ground. The bottle tree stores water in the wood of its trunk. In times of drought, farmers cut up bottle tree trunks and feed them to their cattle to prevent them from dying of thirst.

Australia's national flower is the golden wattle, which belongs to the Acacia family. In spring, the golden wattle produces large clusters of tiny golden flowers. Another striking plant is the flame tree of the coastal rainforests on the Eastern Highlands. From a distance, its bright red flowers create the illusion that the tree is on fire.

It is from the golden wattle that Australia draws its national colors: gold and green. It is the first flower to blossom in spring and has thrived despite bushfires and the harsh conditions.

HISTORY

AUSTRALIA WAS FIRST INHABITED by an indigenous people belonging to the Australoid group, who probably originated from Southeast Asia. These people traveled to the Australian continent about 40,000 years ago, during a period of time when Australia was still joined to the continent of Asia by a string of small islands. These islands acted as huge stepping stones for the early travelers. Sailing south from island to island in canoes and rafts, the Aborigines, as they were later called by Europeans, landed on the north coast of Australia and then moved southward across the rest of the continent.

Although the population of Aborigines had grown to about 300,000 by 1788, British colonists who first arrived in Australia in that year declared the continent *terra nullius*—uninhabited by humans!

Left: **The oldest known remains of Aboriginal people, dating back at least 35,000 years, were discovered at Lake Mungo in New South Wales. One important find is the earliest example of cremation.**

Opposite: **When the British first colonized Australia, they used it as a penal settlement. Criminals were sent by the hundreds to serve their sentence in Australian prisons.**

The first people to settle in Australia were the Aborigines. As they had no written language, rock paintings (*above*) were used to pass their stories from one generation to the other. One interesting Aborigine hunting device is the boomerang (*below*).

NOMADS

Aborigines were nomads living in family clans, each with its own territory where it could camp, hunt, and fish. They burned down large tracts of forest to provide grazing land for giant kangaroos and other animals that are now extinct. They slaughtered and ate them. To help them hunt, the Aborigines brought two useful items from their original homeland: the dingo, a hunting dog that is unique in that it cannot bark, and the boomerang. The latter is a v-shaped wooden wing that can be thrown over great distances. When hurled into the wind, its aerodynamic shape makes it go on an arc-shaped path and eventually come back to the thrower. The boomerang was used to hunt animals.

Aborigines were very effective hunters. The secret of their success lay in their wise use of natural resources. They occupied land in a productive way, moving on with climatic changes and in response to environmental demands. Today, their methods of finding food and water are taught to soldiers, to help them survive in Australia's inhospitable interior. Although they did not build permanent settlements or carry many possessions, they recorded their history and culture in paintings on rocks and caves using charcoal, clay, and ocher. Archeologists have also found evidence of regular contact between Aborigines and Indonesian traders from the north.

TERRA AUSTRALIS INCOGNITA

For many thousands of years, the Aborigines were the only people to visit Australia. Europeans, however, suspected that a "great southern land" existed. Such a land, they reasoned, was needed to balance the weight of the land in the Northern Hemisphere and prevent the world from tipping over! A Greek phrase was used to describe this land: *Terra Australis*

British officers toast the hoisting of the Union Jack on Australian soil, claiming the land for the British Empire.

Incognita—the unknown southern land. This phrase was first used by the Egyptian geographer Ptolemy who, in the second century, sketched a map of the known coasts of Asia and a big unknown piece of land to its south.

Seventeenth century Dutch merchants sailing the trade routes to the East Indies were the first Europeans to set foot in Australia. When the British learned of their reports, they were keen to claim the land for themselves. In 1768, they sent a man on a secret mission. The man's name was James Cook. To the rest of the world, he was preparing to visit Tahiti to observe the planet Venus. But Cook also had other, highly secret orders: to find the southern land and claim it for England. Captain Cook first sighted Australia in April 1770. He spent over a year mapping its east coast, describing its flora and fauna, and attempting to make contact with its natives, the Aborigines.

SETTLING IN

Although news of Cook's voyage caused a sensation in London, more than 10 years passed before the decision was made to establish a colony in Australia. It was to be a penal colony. At that time Britain had a serious and widespread crime problem. The government decided to reduce the terrible overcrowding in jails by a technique known as transportation, which consisted of sending convicted criminals (convicts) to Australia.

The first colony was set up in Sydney Cove in 1788. In the beginning, life was very hard for the new settlers. Their crops did not do well. Their cattle was stolen by the local Aborigines, and food had to be rationed.

Nevertheless, conditions gradually improved and the colony grew. Other settlements were built along the coast of New South Wales and in Tasmania. Between 1788 and 1868, 160,000 convicts were sent to Australia. With them arrived thousands of free settlers, people who chose to escape the poverty and unemployment in Europe and take their chances in Australia. The new migrants increased the status of the colony and encouraged the growth of industry and farming.

By 1859, five colonies (or states) had grown along the coast of Australia. These were: New South Wales, Tasmania, Queensland, Victoria, and South Australia. Each colony had its own governor, laws, trade policies, police, and transportation system. Their relationships with each other were not good. A fierce rivalry existed between the older colonies, and very few people ever visited other colonies.

Australia's vast inland had scarcely been mapped. A number of explorers, some sent by the colonial authorities, set about finding out what lay within the country's enormous interior. The men chosen for these expeditions had to be brave and persevering. They had to travel for months in desolate, unknown country, had to repel attacks from hostile Aborigines, and had to somehow find their way back home! Understandably, many never returned.

The discovery of gold in 1851 caused a frantic gold rush. One year later, 95,000 new arrivals flooded into New South Wales and Victoria.

Elizabeth Beckford, 70, was sentenced to seven years' transportation for stealing 11 pounds of cheese.

James Freeman was condemned to death for robbery when he was 16 years old. The sentence was later changed to seven years' transportation.

James Grace was just 11 years old when he was sentenced to seven years' transportation. He was caught stealing a pair of silk stockings.

Port Arthur in Tasmania was a penal settlement from 1830 to 1877. The prison buildings are very well preserved.

CRIME AND PUNISHMENT

What did a criminal have to do to earn a trip to Australia? Not much, by today's standards. Stealing a buckle or a loaf of bread was enough for a judge to sentence one to a life of exile. Thus Australia became a dumping ground of petty thieves, Irish rebels, and prostitutes.

THE SQUATTERS

Settlers took advantage of the new lands opened up by explorers. They bought flocks of sheep and drove them inland to graze on the newly discovered grasslands. Since these farmers did not buy the land they used, but instead declared their claim to the government, they were called "squatters." "Squatting" was far from easy. Besides the constant threats of drought, bushfire, and flood, squatters had to deal with attacks from Aborigines and armed robbers (bushrangers). Their success depended on how many workers they could find and the constantly changing wool prices in London. Worse than all this was the isolation. Loneliness and boredom sent many men back to the towns to find a bride. The wives of squatters faced a tough life. They had to endure poverty, isolation, and danger. Supplies and mail, often brought by bullock wagon, came a few times a year, weather permitting! Women who could not shoot or ride were scorned and were at a real disadvantage when it came to fending off attacks by Aborigines.

The hard work and sacrifices of the squatters paid off when their wool fetched high prices on the London market. The local "squattocracy" owned comfortable homes and vast areas of land.

Clashes between Aborigines and white settlers became increasingly common. The squatters had taken over the Aborigines' traditional hunting lands. Their nomadic way of life was disrupted and would never again be the same. Since they were unable to get their food the traditional way, the Aborigines fought back by stealing the squatters' sheep. They also attacked the squatters' homes and families. The squatters in turn killed whole tribes of Aboriginal men, women, and children. A century after the First Fleet (the fleet of ships that transported the first settlers to Australia) arrived in Australia, the Aboriginal population had been reduced from 300,000 to 80,000.

THE LEGEND OF NED KELLY

"Edward Kelly, I hereby sentence you to death by hanging. May the Lord have mercy on your soul!" When Ned Kelly, Australia's most famous outlaw and leader of the Kelly Gang, heard these words, he replied to the judge, "Yes, I will meet you there!" Strangely enough, the judge died about two weeks later…

The exploits of this folk hero have been famous in Australia since 1878, when the young horse thief shot a policeman. In the next two years, he and his gang hid out in the Wombat Ranges in Victoria, in between their daring raids on local banks.

Ned's boldest move was to destroy the police train passing through Glenrowan. It also proved to be his undoing. One of his captives managed to escape and warn the police, who soon surrounded the town. For hours nothing stirred. Then, out of the darkness strode a giant figure clad in metal, with guns blazing. Many of the policemen's bullets seemed to bounce off the creature before he collapsed from his wounds. When the policemen looked at the body, they realized that it was Ned Kelly. Ned was wearing an armor made from plough metal. After killing the rest of the gang in a shoot-out, the troopers took Ned Kelly to Melbourne where he was sentenced and hanged on Thursday, November 11, 1880.

THE 20TH CENTURY

On the first day of the 20th century, the states put aside their differences and joined to form the Commonwealth of Australia. Federation and nationhood for the six colonies were not a revolt against the old order, but rather a coming-of-age.

However, like many other countries in the first half of this century, the new nation soon found itself face to face with the double burden of war and depression.

Australia, as a member of the British Empire, automatically followed Great Britain's declaration of war on Germany in 1914. In the next four years, more than 330,000 Australian men volunteered for service in Europe, the Middle East, New Guinea, and the Indian Ocean. On April 25, 1915, Australian soldiers took part in their most famous battle: the Gallipoli campaign. Masterminded by Winston Churchill and involving an army of Australian and New Zealand soldiers (called Anzacs), it proved to be a disaster from the very beginning. Australians, however, celebrate the battle every year on April 25— Anzac Day, the day when Australians first fought for their new nation. Australians will always remember the Anzacs as "the finest body of men brought together in modern times."

The legend of the Anzac dates from 1915, when the heroic troops were defeated by the Turks and Germans.

After the war, Australia opened its doors to migrants from Britain and Europe. For the next 50 years, migrants came to Australia in large numbers. New labor and new markets made the country rich in the 1920s. This period of prosperity ended in 1929 when Australia, along with the United States and many other countries, was plunged into the Great Depression. One of the few bright spots during the years that followed was the opening of Sydney's famous Harbor Bridge. Work on the bridge had started nearly a decade earlier. Over the years, Sydney's inhabitants looked on in wonder as the huge single arch was slowly completed. Despite the hard times, more than 350,000 people flocked to Sydney to catch a glimpse of the bridge when it was declared open in 1932.

World War II, which began in 1939, resulted in closer relations between the United States and Australia. The Australian government, after the invasion of New Guinea by Japan, asked the British for help. Although Britain refused, the United States sent over 100,000 men to Australia. Many Australians believe it was the United States that prevented Australia from being invaded by the Japanese. Twenty years after World War II, Australian

and American soldiers fought together again in Vietnam. The Vietnam War caused much conflict in Australia. Returning soldiers were often booed and hissed at by crowds.

In recent years, Australia's attitude toward communist countries has relaxed. In fact, Australia was the first Western nation to officially recognize the People's Republic of China. Today, many Australian goods are sold to China and the former Soviet Union. Presently, Australia is trying to create closer cultural and economic ties with its neighbors, particularly Southeast Asia and the Pacific Islands. The government spends millions of dollars on foreign aid to countries like the Philippines and Indonesia. Nevertheless, Australia still maintains a strong relationship with the United States as well as its traditional ties with Britain.

In 1988, Australia celebrated its Bicentenary—the 200th anniversary of the arrival of the First Fleet. The celebrations and exhibitions included the World Expo, held in Brisbane. This special year made Australians aware of how far they have progressed in the last 200 years and how much still lies before them.

For the Bicentenary celebrations, Sydney harbor was filled with sailing ships of all shapes and sizes, including a reconstruction of the First Fleet.

29

GOVERNMENT

AUSTRALIA'S FORM OF GOVERNMENT has been described as a constitutional monarchy, in which the queen of England is the nominal head of state. Britain is represented in Australia by the governor-general and six state governors.

FEDERAL GOVERNMENT

Power rests with the elected political party that holds the majority in the House of Representatives. The leader is the prime minister. Government is styled upon the British system of two governing bodies: a legislative assembly (the House of Representatives) and a council of review (the Senate). The Senate consists of 76 members who are elected every six years. The House of Representatives has 147 members and they face elections every three years.

Although Australia's Constitution gives the House of Representatives the right to create laws, they must be passed by the majority of members in the Senate before they become effective. Additionally, any laws that involve changes to the Constitution must be decided by a referendum in which the country's citizens are called to vote on whether or not they want such changes to take place. History has shown that Australians are not eager to alter the Constitution that has served them so well: of the 42 proposals put to a vote in 18 separate referendums, only eight have been passed.

Above: **The new Parliament House fits in very well with Canberra's urban planning.**

SYMBOLS OF A NATION

The national flag consists of a small Union Jack, representing Australia's historical link with Britain; the five stars of the Southern Cross constellation (a permanent feature of the southern hemisphere night sky); and the seven-pointed star, which represents Australia's six States and group of Territories. The Red Ensign is used by merchant ships registered in Australia.

The national coat of arms consists of a shield divided into six sections, each containing a state badge, surrounded by an ermine border, signifying the federation of the states into one nation. The shield is supported by two native animals, an emu (on the right) and a kangaroo, Australia's national animal emblem. They are resting on a branch of golden wattle, Australia's floral emblem.

THE REGIONAL LEVEL

Each of Australia's states is administered by a parliament, which consists of a legislative council (similar to the federal Senate) and a legislative assembly (similar to the House of Representatives). The premier is the leader of the political party dominating the legislative assembly. The state's parliaments existed long before the creation of the federal government and therefore retain many of their former powers. In addition to levying their own taxes and duties, each state runs its own schools and hospitals, administers its own laws, and has its own police force.

Cities and shires (counties) are governed by local councils headed by a mayor. Their responsibilities include town planning, waste management, and road construction.

Each state is self-governing, with its own constitution and parliament. States and territories also have their own court systems. The picture on the left shows the Western Australian coat of arms on the law courts of Perth.

Australians enjoy full democratic rights, including free speech. These protestors are occupying the site of a future uranium mine in South Australia.

PARTICIPATING IN A DEMOCRACY

Australia has a short, but strong, tradition of democracy. Since members of all levels of government are elected, most citizens find themselves visiting a voting booth at least once a year. Unlike in other democracies including the United States, Britain, and France, voting is compulsory for all adult Australians. Citizens who are overseas or otherwise unable to vote in person at a polling center are required to post in an absentee vote. Those who do not vote are fined.

The results of all elections held in Australia are determined using a unique procedure known as the preferential voting system, to ensure that voters have a greater say in whom they elect. Because of the assignment of preferences, the counting of votes may go on for several days before the winner is finally determined. Immediately after an election, members of the ruling party elect a prime minister or premier (usually the leader of the party) and a cabinet of ministers, each responsible for a particular facet of government, such as defense, education, or welfare.

POLITICAL PARTIES

There are currently four major political parties in Australia:

THE AUSTRALIAN LABOR PARTY The nation's oldest party, it was started in 1891 by sheep shearers unhappy with their pay and working conditions. The party of the working people, it has a strong tradition of democratic socialism, pioneering such reforms as pensions and minimum wages. The Labor Party, under Paul Keating's leadership (right), holds the majority in government.

THE LIBERAL PARTY OF AUSTRALIA The party dominated federal politics for two decades after its founding in 1944. Liberals believe in free enterprise and the freedom to conduct their lives with minimum government interference. To this end, they support the reduction of taxes and restrictions on trade and business.

THE NATIONAL PARTY OF AUSTRALIA Known as the National Country Party when it was created in 1919, it is the champion of primary industries such as farming and mining. The party draws its membership primarily from Australia's rural population. For several years now, the National Party and Liberal Party have combined forces in both state and federal parliaments to form ruling coalitions.

THE AUSTRALIAN DEMOCRATS Formed in 1977 by Don Chipp, the party was set up to keep a check on the other major parties, or in the more colorful words of Senator Chipp, "to keep the bastards honest."

THE REPUBLICAN DEBATE

Australians' desire for a republic seems to be growing, especially among the young. The Australian Republican Movement (ARM) argues that changes to the Constitution and the Australian system of democracy should be minimal.

Severing ties with the Commonwealth is also not favored by ARM. Opinion polls have shown that while the majority of Australians are in favor of a republic (as opposed to constitutional monarchy), they are not in favor of adopting the American or French systems. Paul Keating has hinted at a plan to change from constitutional monarchy by January 1, 2001, to mark the anniversary of federation.

ECONOMY

IT IS SAID that Australia's economic fortunes "ride on the sheep's back," in reference to the reliance of the nation's wealth on the exploitation of its natural resources. Australian wool and other agricultural products are well-known throughout the world. Although Australians have traditionally relied on mining and agricultural exports to maintain a standard of living that ranks as one of the highest in the world, international economic trends have brought the realization that continued dependence on primary industry may threaten future prosperity.

Opposite: **Australia's economy has for a long time depended on the export of wool, of which a fine variety is produced by Merino sheep.**

Above: **Livestock is raised in the vast areas of dry inland country. The animals are left to run wild most of the time.**

TRADING PARTNERS

Australia is the world's leading supplier of several important commodities such as aluminium, wool, beef and veal, coal, mineral sands, live goats and sheep, and refined lead.

Australia trades with the developed countries of the world as well as with developing nations. Japan is its biggest customer, buying more than a quarter of all exports. Australia's major exports to Japan are minerals and fuels as well as agricultural products. Another close trading partner is the Southeast Asian region, which accounts for more than a third of Australia's exports. Japan and the United States are Australia's largest suppliers of imports, usually capital equipment. Products from these two countries make up nearly half of all imports. Australia's commitment to developing countries can be seen in the fact that its imports from these countries have increased from less than a sixth to nearly a quarter of its total imports.

The World Trade Centre in Melbourne: Australia is a major player in world trade. For the past few years, it has been trying to diversify its economy to reduce its dependence on agricultural and mining products.

The race is now on to develop other exports that can effectively compete in international markets. To encourage overseas trade and investment, the government in the 1980s restructured the national economy to force domestic industry to become more competitive. The focus of trade was shifted to the rapidly growing markets in Southeast Asia. Attention was also paid to schools and universities to ensure that future graduates were equipped with the necessary skills to aid industry. Long known as the "lucky country" because of its natural wealth, Australia now needs to become, through the hard work and ingenious efforts of its people, the "clever country."

MINERALS AND ENERGY

Australia is a land of incredible mineral wealth. Its deposits of coal, which can satisfy the demands of the whole world for several centuries, is the nation's largest single export earner. Australia is the largest producer of aluminum, most of which is mined along the west coast of the Cape York Peninsula, and the second largest exporter of iron ore. Copper, lead, zinc, gold, and silver are also mined in substantial quantities, along with natural gas, uranium, titanium, and precious gems. Although the income earned from minerals, metals, and fuels accounts for 50% of export earnings and includes the annual export of 81.5 million tons of coal, 88 million tons of iron ore, and 9 million tons of aluminum ore to Japan, Southeast Asia, China, and the European Community, only 0.01% of the continent's reserves has so far been mined.

Australia is one of the world's biggest producers of minerals and metals. Beneath the dry barren soil lies a wealth of minerals and energy resources.

39

BURIED TREASURE

Ninety-five percent of the opals and half of the sapphires that reach the world's markets come from Australia. The world's largest opal mine is near Coober Pedy, a town in South Australia. Because temperatures in the district often exceed 104°F, many of the town's population live in underground homes dug into the dry earth. The Argyle mines in the Kimberley Ranges, Western Australia, produce most of the world's diamonds.

Gold has been mined in great quantities in the states of Victoria, Queensland, Western Australia, and New South Wales since the goldrushes of the 1850s. A number of massive nuggets have been found, including the 205-pound Holtermann nugget and the 78-pound "Welcome Stranger." In 1931, the body of Harold Lasseter was found in the Northern Territory. Lasseter had earlier claimed to have found a fabulous mile-long reef of gold. Although a number of adventurers have later tried (and failed) to find Lasseter's Reef, it is widely believed that the reef and its incredible wealth do exist and are waiting—somewhere in the Outback—to be found.

AGRICULTURE

Despite the arid soils and dry climate, agricultural exports, including wheat, wool, beef, sugar, and dairy products, earn approximately a third of Australia's income. This is in part due to the limited domestic demand of the nation's small population and the application of extensive farming techniques to semi-arid lands. Sheep ranches (known as "stations") in Australia's inland, for example, stock 12 head of sheep for every square mile. Such stations are tens of thousands of acres in size. Most of Australia's 150 million sheep are raised for their wool.

Because of Australia's unpredictable climate and the continual fluctuation in international demand for agricultural products, the volume and value of Australia's agricultural produce vary greatly from year to year. The nation's farmers cope with the unpredictable market by rapidly changing to new crops and livestock as the need arises. Nevertheless the influence of trade blocs, price slumps, high domestic interest rates, and rising costs has created a serious financial crisis in Australia's rural sector, once said to be the most efficient in the world.

With the help of modern equipment, farmers are able to harvest substantial quantities of grain. Wheat is one of the main crops.

Mineral- and metal-processing is greatly expanding, with mineral sands-processing and aluminum production leading the way.

MANUFACTURING

In addition to its steel works and aluminum smelters, Australia's major manufacturing industries include clothing and textiles, chemicals, aeronautical equipment, and electronics. The local motor vehicle industry produces 3 million cars a year. Four of the largest international passenger motor vehicle builders—Ford, General Motors, Mitsubishi, and Toyota—have manufacturing facilities in Australia, producing more than 300,000 units a year.

TOURISM

In recent years, Australia has been riding the crest of an unprecedented wave of popularity among international travelers. More than 2 million tourists visit Australia annually, spending millions of dollars during their stay. Revenue from tourism comes to $2.7 billion every year. It is the largest industry in Australia, providing directly or indirectly more than 441,000 jobs. Most visitors come from the United States and New Zealand, as well as Britain, Germany, and Japan.

Australia is one of the world's most attractive countries to visit. Most visitors make it a point to go to Ayers Rock, now sometimes referred to by it's original name, "Uluru."

TOURISM'S BAKER'S DOZEN

Australia's 13 most popular tourist attractions for overseas visitors are:
1. Sydney Opera House and Rocks area, Sydney
2. Darling Harbor, Sydney
3. Sydney Harbor and beaches, Sydney
4. Sydney Tower, Sydney
5. Surfers Paradise, Gold Coast
6. The Blue Mountains, New South Wales
7. Taronga Park Zoo, Sydney
8. Queen Victoria Markets, Melbourne
9. New South Wales Art Gallery and Museum, Sydney
10. Royal Botanical Gardens, Melbourne
11. Seaworld, Gold Coast
12. King's Park, Perth
13. Jupiter's Casino, Gold Coast

AUSTRALIANS

LURED BY OPPORTUNITIES of wealth and freedom in the "lucky country," Australia has been a favorite destination for migrants from all parts of the world. Each year, about 100,000 settlers come to Australia, adding to a population that numbered 17.5 million in 1992. Although most migrants still come from Britain, considerable numbers have arrived from other European nations and, in recent years, from Asia.

Today, one in three Australians was born overseas or has a parent who was born overseas. Australia's traditional British heritage is now giving way to a richer, multicultural society—a melting pot of peoples from more than 100 ethnic backgrounds, speaking 90 different languages and practicing over 80 separate religions.

Left: **Australia is a migrant society. For this migrant family, citizenship day is the most important day in their lives and the certificate of citizenship a most precious document.**

Opposite: **After a steady decline, the Aboriginal population has started to increase in the last seven years.**

POPULATION DISTRIBUTION

Surprisingly, Australia is one of the most highly urbanized countries in the world. Eighty-five percent of the country's population—about 15 million people—live in cities and large towns, mostly in Sydney, Melbourne, and Brisbane, the nation's three largest capital cities. Sydney, the capital of New South Wales, is Australia's largest city, with a population of 3.7 million. Melbourne is only slightly less populated, with 3.1 million inhabitants. The third largest is Brisbane, with more than 1.3 million residents. Australia's farmers, responsible for much of the nation's wealth, make up less than 1% of the population.

Currently, about 40% of all Australians are under 25 years of age, but this proportion is expected to become progressively lower because of long life expectancies (74 years for men and 80 years for women) and low birth rates. The growing number of older people in the country is expected to put extra demands on health services and public welfare in the near future as the relative size of Australia's 8.6 million-strong workforce dwindles. Although Australians pride themselves on being a nation of athletes, a diet high in meat has taken its toll on their health. Figures vary, but it is estimated that nearly one in two people is overweight, a contributing factor to the major causes of death: heart disease, cancer, and strokes.

Australia is a young nation, and all children dream of becoming great sportsmen.

The Chinese community celebrates Chinese New Year through Sydney's Chinatown with lion dances and great rejoicing.

BUILDING A MULTICULTURAL SOCIETY

In the last century, Australians saw themselves as "98% British." The white population was overwhelmingly Anglo-Saxon and Celtic, descendants of convicts and settlers from England and Ireland. In addition to doubling the nation's population within a matter of a few years, the goldrushes of the 1850s brought migrants from a variety of ethnic backgrounds, including many Chinese. Although a large number returned to their homeland after the gold trickled out, others chose to stay. Descendants of Chinese workers (known as "ABCs" or "Australian Born Chinese") have lived in Australia for several generations as evidenced by their large and well-organized communities in the capital cities. Chinese food has also become entrenched in Australian culture: nearly every town, large or small, boasts a Chinese restaurant.

The arrival of the early migrants caused concern among much of the population, leading to the enactment in 1901 of the "White Australia" immigration policy designed to exclude non-European migrants. This policy was only replaced in 1973. The large wave of migrants coming to the country at the end of World War II was therefore mainly from Europe, in particular from Italy, Greece, Yugoslavia, and Germany. The first Asian people to settle in Australia from the mid-1970s onward were Vietnamese "boat people"—refugees fleeing the communist regime in their homeland. Since then, considerable numbers of migrants have come from Southeast Asia, India, the Philippines, Japan, China, and Hong Kong. They have brought much needed money and valuable skills to the nation. Racism is no longer a part of the Australian's attitude toward Asian migrants.

For a long time, the "White Australia" policy discriminated against non-white migrants. However, the country is now truly on its way to building a multiracial society.

OLD PEOPLE IN A NEW LAND

In 1988, while most of the population were celebrating the 200th anniversary of European settlement in Australia, a section of the community declared a year of mourning. They were Australia's original inhabitants, the Aborigines. Like the indigenous peoples of many other countries, Aborigines were originally subjected to many injustices by European settlers and were later forced to abandon their culture to adapt to a European-style society. Few have successfully managed to make this transition, and today Australia's 250,000 Aborigines have the highest rate of unemployment, the greatest threat of disease, and the lowest level of education in the country. They also commit the most crimes of any ethnic group in the nation.

About half of them live in the towns and cities and have adopted an urban lifestyle. However, most of them remain poor, and Aboriginal people are the single most disadvantaged group in Australia.

After years of "assimilation," Aborigines are now encouraged to preserve and reinforce their unique cultural identity.

The "Aborigine question" has polarized Australian society. Those who believe that the problems faced by the Aboriginal community were caused by unfair treatment by Europeans in the past include many members of recent governments. Of the many public programs and incentives instituted to help Aborigines, one in particular—the giving of land held sacred by the Aboriginal community back to the Aborigines—has been enormously controversial. Opponents of the so-called "land rights" legislation claim that Australia belongs to all Australians, not just to one particular section of the community. They also point to instances of mismanagement of land already given to Aboriginal groups, including the subsequent selling of sacred land to mining interests.

One of the reasons the "Aborigine question" has caused so much argument among the community is that it cuts to the very heart of two ideals held very dearly by Australians: admiration for the "battler," the underdog fighting the establishment, and the belief that everyone deserves a "fair go," the right to compete equally with others.

Through the "land rights" program, the government aims to restore land ownership to Aborigines.

A NEED FOR KNOWLEDGE AND IDENTITY

University lecturer and author James Miller believes the Aborigines would be greatly assisted by raising the level of their education and instilling a sense of identity within their community. An Aborigine himself, he prefers to be known as a "Koori."

"I use the term 'Koori' because it's my ancestral form of identification. Also, 19th century thinking portrayed my people as simple, barbaric and savage, using the term 'aboriginal,' and we were not those things. I really can't identify with it because it doesn't give my people a separate identity."

LIFESTYLE

"RELAXED AND FRIENDLY" is the Australian image made famous throughout the world by comedian and actor Paul Hogan, and to a large extent, this description holds true. Despite the pressures of a modern Western society, Australians retain the old-fashioned values of hospitality, honesty, and modesty.

Australians have been described as belonging to "the 51st state of the United States" because of their close identification with American culture. This stemmed from the arrival of thousands of American troops in the country during World War II. In addition to American influences seen in fashion, food, and entertainment, the Australian lifestyle is also shaped by Europe and, more recently, Asia.

Left: **The typical Aussie is a warm, smiling individual who still clings to the old-fashioned values of hospitality, honesty and modesty.**

Opposite: **Australians are a fun-loving, colorful people. "Relaxed and friendly" aptly describes the Australian way of life.**

LESSONS FROM THE SWAGMAN

During the depths of the Great Depression of the 1930s, thousands of Australians, out of work and out of money, threw a few belongings in a bag (or "swag"), bid farewell to their families, and headed for the Outback in search of work. From these men grew the tradition of the "swagman." The swagman embodies many of the following ideals that Australians greatly admire, ideals that influence Australian lives and attitudes.

- Mateship refers to the bonds between close friends (referred to as "mates"). These bonds are extraordinarily strong among Australians. Mates are expected to look after each other in times of need: failure to do so—letting down a mate—is considered a great shame in Australia.

- "A fair go" refers to the belief that all individuals, regardless of birth or background, should be given an equal chance to succeed in what they choose to do.

- The imagination of the Australian public is captured by stories of "battlers," or underdogs, who fight against overwhelming odds. But, although Australians are ever willing to help those in need, they also like to see individuals who flaunt their success to be "brought down a peg or two." This is known as the "Tall Poppy Syndrome."

- The "larrikan," or the rogue with a heart of gold, has a special place in Australian hearts. Famous larrikans include actor and comedian Paul Hogan, Bob Hawke, prime minister of Australia in the 1980s and 1990s, and Ginger Meggs, a popular cartoon character.

THE FAMILY

Like the people in other Western societies, Australians live in nuclear families made up of parents, brothers, and sisters. Because of the vastness of the continent and the willingness of the population to travel in search of work or a better lifestyle, contact between members of the extended family—grandparents, uncles, aunts, and cousins—is infrequent. Family members do, however, get together at Christmas and Easter, often traveling thousands of miles across the country to share in the celebrations and catch up on family gossip.

From an early age, children are taught to be independent and self-sufficient. Dating begins in the early teens, and many teenagers are working and living away from home by the time they are 16. Although the law recognizes youths over the age of 18 as adults by giving them the right to vote, the 21st birthday is celebrated as the day of coming into adulthood. During the course of the celebrations (which can often be quite elaborate), the birthday boy or girl is presented with a symbolic key representing the beginning of a new and independent life. Festivities are usually accompanied by much drinking, embarrassing speeches, and elaborate pranks, much to the amusement of all present.

Outback recreation stresses family activity. Despite the emphasis on independence and self-reliance, the family unit is still a strong pillar of society.

EDUCATION

All children between six and 15 years (16 in Tasmania) of age must attend school. After the first six or seven years of primary school, pupils progress to high school where they spend a minimum of four years. Those intending to go on to college or further advance their education spend an extra two years in high school in preparation for a public examination. The nature of this final school examination varies from state to state.

The school day generally runs from 9 a.m. to 3:30 p.m., with breaks of half an hour for morning tea and an hour for lunch. Extracurricular activities like sports and debating may keep children at school in the afternoons or on weekends. Education is free, unless parents decide to send their children to private schools. Annual fees at private schools range from under $750 for institutions run by the Catholic Church to over $10,000 at the nation's top boarding schools. Although the wearing of uniforms is compulsory at private schools, this is usually not the case with government-run schools.

Students electing to further their education have a choice of going to a university or enrolling in vocational training at a technical college, known as a TAFE—which stands for Technical and Further Education. Most students spend three years in college to obtain an arts or science degree. Those studying for the professions may spend up to six years obtaining their qualifications. Government and industry provide scholarships to help students of outstanding merit.

Australian education may be described as progressive. Instead of merely teaching the three R's (reading, 'riting and 'rithmetic), pupils are encouraged to think, to question, and to argue the merits of existing beliefs. Emphasis is placed on the teaching of skills that will assist students in the adult world and encourage them to make a mature contribution to society.

Every year, the federal government increases its expenditure on education by 10%, to make available the latest educational aids and technical equipment.

The School System

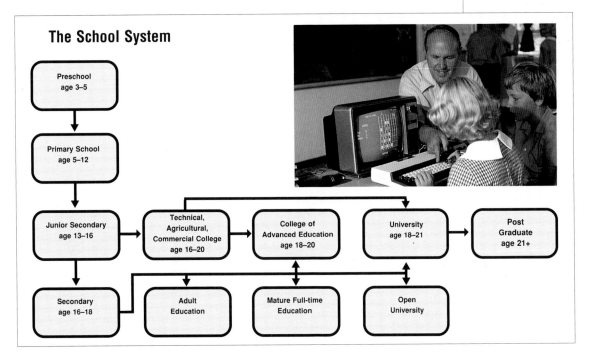

THE SCHOOL OF THE AIR

Children in Australia's isolated Outback unable to attend a regular school can instead take part in the School of the Air. A service run by state governments, the School of the Air broadcasts lessons over the air. Students participate in discussions with teachers and classmates using a two-way radio. Tests and projects are supervised by parents and mailed to the School. Because of the great distances that often exist between teachers and students, many students of the School of the Air never meet their teachers or classmates in person. To help children with their studies, Outback parents may also employ "home tutors," similar to the governesses of the past.

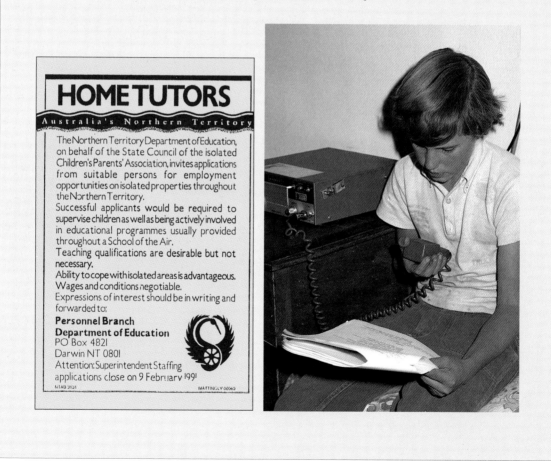

HOME TUTORS
Australia's Northern Territory

The Northern Territory Department of Education, on behalf of the State Council of the isolated Children's Parents' Association, invites applications from suitable persons for employment opportunities on isolated properties throughout the Northern Territory.

Successful applicants would be required to supervise children as well as being actively involved in educational programmes usually provided throughout a School of the Air.

Teaching qualifications are desirable but not necessary.

Ability to cope with isolated areas is advantageous. Wages and conditions negotiable.

Expressions of interest should be in writing and forwarded to:

Personnel Branch
Department of Education
PO Box 4821
Darwin NT 0801
Attention: Superintendent Staffing
applications close on 9 February 1991

NTAB 3131   MATTINGLY 00560

WORK

It used to be the case in most families that the husband worked and the wife stayed at home to look after the house and see to the children. Changing attitudes and the rising cost of living have, however, encouraged women to return to work. Today, 51% of Australia's workforce are women, and this proportion is increasing. Two-thirds of all the Australian workforce is employed in the service industry, which includes retailing, health, entertainment, education, and finance. It also includes Australia's largest employer, the Public Service, which employs one in four Australians.

In the past, long and hard battles were fought for the conditions enjoyed by workers today. Among the innovations now offered by most employers are flexitime in which workers can choose the hours they work, a minimum wage in proportion to the work involved, and retirement programs to support workers when they stop working. In addition, employers must observe strict anti-discrimination laws which prevent job applicants from being rejected on the basis of race, sex, age, or physical disability. Workers' rights are further protected by unions, which are strong and well-organized. There are 275 trade unions, and one out of every two workers belongs to a union. More than 150 unions are affiliated with the Australian Council of Trade Unions, representing about 2.4 million workers.

The average Australian wage earner works seven to eight hours a day, Monday to Friday, and have four weeks' paid vacation a year. The labor force consists of more than two-thirds of the civilian population aged 15 and over.

AN ORDINARY DAY

Most Australians lead an urban lifestyle. From Monday to Friday the urban Aussie wakes up around 7 a.m. After a breakfast of juice, cereal, toast, and/or eggs and bacon, family members go their various ways to start work or attend school.

The children attend school from about 9 a.m. to 3:30 p.m. and adults work from 9 a.m. to 5 p.m. The family gathers together for dinner at about 6:30 p.m. After dinner, the children do their homework and their parents might read or watch television. Most suburban families are in bed by 10 p.m. during the week.

On the weekend, the Australian family takes part in some form of recreation, which can include a simple barbecue in the backyard with close friends, or a drive to the countryside with a picnic or barbecue lunch. Being sports lovers, the Australian family may either pursue a favorite sport or watch it on television.

Elderly people live in their own homes, and the family visits the grandparents on weekends.

THE GREAT AUSTRALIAN DREAM

The most popular dwellings in Australia are free-standing houses built of brick with a tile roof, usually situated on a quarter acre of land. Most houses have at least three bedrooms, a living room, kitchen and dining area, and a family or "rumpus" room. Homes in warmer areas have open verandas that may run the length of the house. Families often sleep on the veranda on hot nights to take advantage of cool breezes. Many houses in the tropics are built on stilts. In addition to allowing better circulation of air, this feature also protects the home from floods.

The desire to own a house on a plot of land is known as the "Great Australian Dream." Although this goal does not seem particularly ambitious, it is becoming increasingly harder to realize as Australia's urban landscape becomes more congested. City dwellers in particular often have to settle for rented high-rise apartments or old semi-detached cottages. The prices of these dwellings have skyrocketed in recent years, placing them well out of the reach of the average income earner. Nevertheless, three in four families own their homes.

RELIGION

THE VARIOUS RELIGIOUS GROUPS in Australia are not confined to particular geographical regions. Because Australia is a secular state with no official national religion, followers of all religions are free to practice their activities under the full protection of the law. It is true to say, however, that the law is seldom required to settle religious disputes, which are kept to a minimum, due to the easygoing nature of the Australian people.

As the Australian population is made up of peoples with different backgrounds, there is also a wide variety of religions and places of worship. Immigrants are encouraged to keep their own cultures, and religious practice is viewed with tolerance, both by the government and the population. Christianity is the major religion, but Judaism, Islam and Buddhism also have many followers. In addition, religious sects—both Christian and non-Christian—also enjoy quite a following.

Although over three-quarters of the population describe themselves as Christians, only one out of four attends church on a regular basis. The Church nevertheless plays an important role in society, carrying out charity work and organizing social gatherings.

There are various religions in Australia. Evidence of the population's tolerance is the wide distribution of different places of worship. Both the Baha'i temple (*opposite*) and the Sze-Yup Buddhist Temple (*above*) are in Sydney.

Three-quarters of the population profess Christianity. One third of all Christians are Anglican and another third are Catholics.

THE CHRISTIAN CHURCHES

Also known as the Church of England, the Anglican Church was the first organized religion in Australia and has therefore played a dominant role in shaping the nation's legal, social, and political institutions. Anglicans believe that religion cannot be separated from everyday life, and church leaders have a reputation for speaking out on social issues.

Australia's other major Christian denomination, Roman Catholicism, was first introduced by Irish migrants settling in Australia early in the 19th century. More recent migrants from Italy and Asia have strengthened the Church's numbers; today, one in three Australians is a Roman Catholic. Although this represents more than 4 million followers, the Roman Catholic Church has no Australian cardinal. Local policies of the Church are instead decided by a council of bishops.

The Christian Churches

Roman Catholics and Anglicans make up about two-thirds of all Christians in Australia. The remainder are mainly Presbyterians, Methodists, Lutherans, Baptists, and followers of the Eastern Orthodox Church. The Presbyterian Church is noted for its charity and missionary work. Its assistance projects include the Flying Doctor Service that brings rapid medical attention to isolated families in outback Queensland. Several minor churches have combined to form the Uniting Church.

One unique Outback institution is the Flying Doctor service. A project initiated by the Presbyterian Church, it brings medical assistance to people of all religious faiths.

Sydney's Buddhist adherents are drawn from its large community of Chinese and other Asians.

THE FLOGGING PARSON

Among the first Anglican leaders in Australia was the Reverend Samuel Marsden. On arriving in Australia in 1794 at the age of 29, he was confronted with a colony in chaos. Drunkenness and corruption were rife, especially among the settlement's soldiers who were paid in rum because of the absence of proper currency. Determined to instill order and a proper regard for the Church, Marsden immediately set about building a church to preach his sermons warning of the wrath of God. When in public, the Anglican priest carried a large whip that he did not hesitate to use on unlucky passers-by.

It was in his role as the colony's magistrate that Marsden gained his title of "the flogging parson." Prisoners from an ill-fated convict rebellion were flogged by the priest to extract confessions. Then, after sentencing them in court, Marsden would remove his magisterial robes to personally administer the punishment, which invariably consisted of a brutal flogging. But, despite his fearsome reputation, Marsden is also remembered as a visionary who helped establish the wool industry and fostered the growth of the Anglican Church in Australia.

THE SIKHS OF WOOLGOOLGA

Visitors to the coastal town of Woolgoolga cannot miss the domed white building overlooking the town. On closer inspection, they will see a notice instructing visitors to remove their shoes and cover their heads with a handkerchief before entering. This temple, known as the Guru Nanak Sikh Gurdwara, was built by the city's community of Sikhs, which make up about a third of the town's population. Sikhs first settled in Woolgoolga earlier this century to grow banana trees, which can be seen rising from the surrounding hills.

Guru Nanak, after whom the temple is named, was the founder of Sikhism in the 16th century. Sikhism is a fusion of the tenets of Hinduism and Islam. Sikhs have adopted five objects as a mark of their religion: long hair, short trousers, a comb, an iron bangle, and a dagger.

The belief in one god is a basic tenet of Sikh scripture. Devout Sikhs express their worship in three ways: daily recitation of set passages of scripture, daily family worship, and regular attendance at the temple.

In the 1986 census, 73% of Australians said they were Christians, 12.7% said they were non-religious and 12.3% did not reply.

NON-CHRISTIAN RELIGIONS

The 13% of Australians belonging to non-Christian religions include followers of Judaism, Hinduism, and Islam.

JUDAISM Australian Jews generally take a liberal interpretation of the 613 commandments that make up Jewish Law, but strictly adhere to their three main religious observances: Rosh Hashana (New Year), Yom Kippur (The Day of Atonement), and Passover.

HINDUISM Australia's Hindus come mainly from India and East Africa. The Hindu religion puts a lot of importance on ritual and every stage of an individual's life is marked by a ceremony.

Of all religious minorities, Islam is the fastest growing one. Australia's Moslem immigrants, although abiding by Australian law, have retained their traditional costumes and religious rituals.

ISLAM   Islam is one of the fastest growing religions in Australia. Introduced by Afghan cameliers who were brought to Australia by the early explorers, the Moslem religion is founded on the Five Pillars of Islam: the worship of Allah and the belief that Mohammad was the last prophet, daily prayers, fasting, charity, and pilgrimage to Mecca. Like Judaism, Australian Islam is of a liberal brand, although devotees abide by the rules of their faith, say their prayers regularly, and set aside part of their income for charity. Moslem law is not officially recognized by the government.

ABORIGINAL RELIGION

Aboriginal religion centers on a supernatural world known as the Dreamtime or The Dreaming. They believe that this world existed long before the coming of man and still continues to exist in parallel with ordinary life. The creation of the world by spirits and creatures from the Dreamtime is told in stories passed down from generation to generation and in Aboriginal art and dance.

Aboriginal belief can be described as a sophisticated form of animism. Tribes have adopted local plants, animals, and features of the landscape as sacred totems, the most important being Uluru—the Aboriginal name for central Australia's Ayers Rock. Uluru is believed to be the spiritual center of Australia, and the source of numerous spiritual forces permeating the country. Sacred sites like Uluru are used to increase the power of Dreamtime magic. One of the most potent magic spells is "pointing the bone," in which an unlucky victim is sung to death by a medicine man in an elaborate ceremony. The victim's only hope of escape is to persuade a more powerful medicine man to reverse the spell. Today, "pointing the bone" survives as a figure of speech meaning "to accuse."

Ayers Rock (Uluru to the Aborigines, and now the official name) is the largest rock on earth. It is about 1.5 miles long and 1,000 feet high. The Aborigines consider it to have a special spiritual significance.

69

LANGUAGE

AUSTRALIANS SPEAK ENGLISH, but a form of English rich in colorful slang and words borrowed from Aboriginal dialects. While very similar to the language spoken in other English-speaking countries, Australian English contains subtleties only fully appreciated by those who have had a long acquaintance with the language.

In its written form, Australian English combines elements of British and American language. Standard spellings and meanings of words are listed in the Macquarie Dictionary. The names of Australia's unique flora and fauna, its geographical features and cities were often adopted from local Aboriginal words. Moreover, some of Australia's pioneers were obviously hard pressed to find names for their new discoveries. Explorer Ernest Giles named a newly found group of magnificent mountains "The Ophthalmia Range," after a disease that was plaguing him at the time!

Left: **Written English is much the same as elsewhere in the world.**

Opposite: **Australians keep a friendly distance when talking to each other, but do not touch. The hands are usually kept behind the back.**

CONVERSATION

By placing the tongue in a low position in the mouth when pronouncing groups of vowels (known technically as diphthongs), you can produce the distinctive "broad" Australian accent. "Day" is pronounced as "dai" and "die" as "doi." The broad Australian accent is spoken throughout the country and gives Australian conversation a flavor of its own.

Inhabitants of other English-speaking countries have in the past not taken well to the Australian accent. Local film makers often had to dub or subtitle their work in response to complaints from foreign audiences. In 1911, one English author went so far to say that "the common speech of the Commonwealth of Australia represents the most brutal maltreatment which has ever been inflicted on the mother tongue of the great English-speaking nations." Harsh words indeed!

THE AUSTRALIAN UNDERSTATEMENT

Making little of major occurrences is a distinguishing feature of Australian conversation. As Australians generally lead a leisurely lifestyle, they tend to make light of events that might be considered important in other societies. They do not like to over-dramatize, unless telling one of their tall stories. In this case, everything is blown out of all proportion. However, understatement is the more usual feature.

Districts beset by tremendous gale force winds and torrential rains are "having a spot of bad weather." People in serious trouble are described as "having a bit of bother" and those who have achieved outstanding success have "done all right."

"Some trouble with a steer:" the caption to this drawing is a perfect example of the typical Australian understatement.

A CRASH COURSE IN AUSTRALIAN ENGLISH

Visitors who wish to pass as authentic Australians should follow these simple rules:

- The greeting: Most Australians greet people with "G'day" (Good Day). If people are in a good mood or meeting a friend, "G'day mate!" is used. "Mate" (friend) is used extensively in conversation, usually at the end of a phrase. The greeting may also be accompanied by "The Australian Salute," a casual wave of the hand across the face to keep the flies away.
- Speak slowly: Australian conversation is similar to Australian lifestyle—relaxed. Locals are suspicious of "fast talkers," whom they see as trying to "pull a fast one" (play a trick).
- Smile frequently: Being a naturally friendly people, Australians accompany their conversations with smiles. Talkers who don't smile are assumed to be in "a spot of trouble."
- Keep gestures to a minimum: While talking, the body should be in a casual slouch with arms folded. Talkers who use frequent or elaborate hand gestures run the risk of being labeled a "fast talker." Touching makes Australians feel uncomfortable and should be avoided.
- Putting it all together: For the finishing touch, conversations should be dotted by common phrases such as "Fair dinkum?" (Is that a fact?) or "She'll be right" (It's under control).

AUSTRALIAN SLANG

Much of Australia's colorful slang dates back to the country's early days. For example, "bludger," a criticism leveled at those who are lazy, owes its origins to the early colony's ruthless muggers, who struck their victims with heavy sticks (bludgeons) before making away with their possessions.

Local farmers are known as "cockies," short for "cockatoo growers," since after spending a hard day sowing a field, a farmer would often wake up the next morning to find a flock of cockatoos, or Australian parrots, busily eating all his seeds. The farmer would "get his own back" by indulging in a meal of "bush mutton," or roast cockatoo! The galah, a species of cockatoo, has a reputation for being incredibly stupid. Thousands of galahs are killed each year because of their astonishing habit of pecking at live power lines. Silly people are good-naturedly referred to as "galahs."

Nicknames are an affectionate tradition in Australia. Usually, friends' names are shortened by adding an "o" to the end of the first syllable. "David" becomes "Davo" and "John" becomes "Johnno." The "o" ending is also used for other things such as coffee breaks, known as "smokos."

Australian speech is flavored with slang and colloquialism, which are in keeping with the nation's character.

Many Aboriginal languages have been irretrievably lost, a tragic circumstance, as Aboriginal tradition and culture depended solely on oral—not written—transmission.

ABORIGINAL LANGUAGE

The various Aboriginal tribes in Australia originally spoke between them about 250 languages that comprised as many as 700 dialects. These languages were separate languages, each as distinct from each other as Chinese from Greek. None of the languages had a written script.

European contact wiped out several of the Aboriginal languages. At least 50 were unfortunately lost forever. In the case of 100 other languages, the number of speakers is so small and the records so inadequate that the language will die with them. Only about 50 languages are regarded as "strong." Even then, only 20 of them are spoken by "large" groups of about 500 people.

Aboriginal languages are characterized by great similarities in their sounds and a fairly common grammatical structure, but by few similarities in vocabulary. Nevertheless, there are some common words found in many of these languages—nouns such as "jina" meaning foot and "mayi" meaning vegetable.

BLOKES, BLOWIES AND BLUES

Some common words and phrases used by Australians:

Avago y'mug! ("Have a go, you mug"): A frustrated plea to people ("mugs") who are not trying hard enough. Used often at sporting events.

Back of Bourke: Australia's inland, or Outback.

Bloke: A person, used in the same way as *guy* in the United States.

Blowie: A blowfly. Mosquitoes are referred as *mozzies*.

Blue: An argument.

Bonza or *beaut*: Good.

Chook: A chicken, as in "running round like a chook with its head cut off," a phrase used to describe people in a panic.

Dobber: An informant.

Drongo or *nong*: Idiot.

Dunny: Toilet.

Fair crack of the whip: A plea for leniency.

Kangaroos in his top paddock: Not of sound mind.

Nipper: A young child, also known as an ankle biter.

Oz: Australia. Australians call themselves *Aussies*.

Pom or *Pommie*: An Englishman.

Stone the crows: An expression of surprise.

Tinnie: A beer can. Alcohol, *grog* or *plonk*, is drunk at pubs (bars).

Yobbos: Hooligans, also known as *hoons* and *ratbags*.

"I bin luk kwesjin mat" means "He was amazed" in Aboriginal Kriol.

Early European contacts recorded some words in the local language called Dharuk. They included a number of words that have since been adopted into Australian English, such as "dingo," now used as the name for a wild dog.

For a long time, Aboriginal children attended schools where English was spoken, but in the early 1970s, bilingual education was introduced for some Aboriginal communities. Language centers have been set up to keep alive the Aboriginal languages. As time has passed, Aborigines have also incorporated some English words into their language. One such Aboriginal language is Kriol.

NEWSPAPERS

Australians are avid readers of newspapers and love listening to the radio. They buy about 4.5 million newspapers each day and about 3 million on Sunday. The Australian press is free to express its views and opinions with very little censorship from the government. Most newspapers have achieved a high standard of reporting, especially such papers as the *Sydney Morning Herald* and the *Melbourne Age*. Both these papers date from the mid-19th century.

Most newspapers circulate only in the state where they are published: *The Daily Telegraph* in New South Wales, *The Age* in Victoria, and *The Courier Mail* in Queensland. Each state capital has at least one morning and one afternoon newspaper.

Right: **Australians read more newspapers than any other nation in the world. Most papers are regional, only two having national circulation.**

Opposite: **Radio Australia broadcasts in a variety of languages to cater to ethnic minorities.**

In 1964, a national newspaper called *The Australian* was founded, and is sold throughout Australia. The *Australian Financial Review* also has a national readership. Australia has several foreign language newspapers, with the largest circulation in Sydney and Melbourne. Greek and Italian migrants have the largest number of foreign newspapers.

There are also several periodicals popular with all Australians. *The Bulletin*, founded in 1880, reflects national thought and beliefs, while the *Australian Women's Weekly*, founded in 1933, has a wide readership among Australian women. There are 150 publications in 40 languages.

RADIO AND TELEVISION

Broadcasting and television are shared between the government-sponsored Australian Broadcasting Corporation (ABC) and a number of commercial stations. In the mid-1970s, a special service was introduced to provide programs in foreign languages for the benefit of Australia's ethnic communities. It is operated by the Special Broadcasting Service (SBS) and funded by the federal government.

ARTS

THE EARLIEST EXAMPLES of art in Australia date back tens of thousands of years. Created by Aboriginal artists, these sculptures and cave paintings illustrate a mythical age when strange spirits and fantastic beasts roamed a young landscape. This period, called Dreamtime or Dreaming, is also celebrated in Aboriginal songs and sacred ceremonies called *corroborees*, in which dancers paint Dreamtime symbols on their bodies. The dancers are led by musicians who beat clap-sticks or play the *didgeridoo*, a long hollow pipe made from a tree log.

Opposite: **The Melbourne Arts Centre nestles in a clump of luxuriant vegetation.**

Below: **A group of Aborigines perform the *corroboree* for spectators. The word is commonly used to refer to a combined performance of music and dance.**

DESCRIBING THE LANDSCAPE

The Australian government gives full support to local artists. Artbank was created in 1980 to stimulate a greater appreciation of Australian art.

Australia's numerous art galleries are favorite attractions for both local and overseas visitors. They exhibit a diverse collection of both local and international art, including a number of works that have won the nation's most prestigious art award—the Archibald Prize. Among the winning works are several landscape paintings. Painting the unique Australian landscape presented a major challenge to early European artists, who soon found themselves discarding the styles and rules they had learned in their homelands.

The 1880s saw a new breed of landscape artists rising to the challenge. Rejecting the guidelines that were established by painters in the past, these artists, called Impressionists, succeeded in capturing the essence of the country and its people in paintings of simple, everyday scenes. The lessons learned by the Australian Impressionists were adopted by future artists such as Norman Lindsay, who in addition to painting, wrote several books including *The Magic Pudding*—a tale well known to all Australian children. *Ned Kelly*, painted by Sidney Nolan, has become as famous as Tom Roberts' *Shearing the Rams*. His

Aboriginal art makes use of bright, warm colors and unusual shapes to convey their relationship with the land and its spirits. Here is pictured **Pro Hart**, a modern landscape artist.

works, along with those of a growing number of modern Australian artists, are becoming increasingly admired overseas.

The Australian National Gallery in Canberra is world renowned for its collection of Australian art, particularly Aboriginal art. The National Gallery of Victoria also exhibits the works of world-famous artists.

A DREAMTIME STORY: *WHY THE STARS TWINKLE*

One night, a long time ago, some women went out to dig for yams. They dug and dug with their digging sticks. Some were lucky and found lots of yams. Others did not find any. After returning to camp, those who had yams cooked them over a fire.

The women who did not find any yams felt ashamed. They decided to live in the sky so that people all around the world could see them. But as they were rising up to the sky, the women who were eating their yams rushed to join them and went up too.

All the women turned into stars. On a clear night you can see them. The stars of those who did not find any yams are still and dim. But the lucky ones, the ones who found yams, twinkle as they eat their yams.

–from the Maung tribe of the Northern Territory

A SCULPTURE THAT SINGS

The largest sculpture in Australia is 597 feet wide and 221 feet high. One hundred and fifty tons of concrete, 66,420 square feet of glass, 84 miles of high tension steel cable, and 1,056,000 tiles were used in its construction. It took nearly 20 years to build and cost $77 million. Within the 10 huge concrete shells that soar from its base are more than 900 rooms, including a concert hall that seats nearly 3,000 people, an opera theater, a library, and two restaurants.

The sculpture is in fact a building: the Sydney Opera House, one of the wonders of modern architecture. It was conceived in 1955, when the New South Wales state government issued a challenge to the world's best architects to design an opera house fit for its capital, Sydney. The task was very difficult: the winning design was to be located on a narrow strip of land jutting out into the city harbor. It was to have two concert halls, capable of seating 1,000 and 3,000 people each. Above all, the building had to be beautiful.

The competition was won by Jorn Utzon, an architect who lived halfway across the world in Norway. His vision of huge concrete shells soaring above the harbor like the white sails of a giant sailing ship captured the imagination of both the judges and the public. Building Utzon's dream was much more difficult, since engineers were afraid that the hall's shells would collapse under strong winds. Money, too, was a problem. In an effort to raise funds for the building's construction, Sydney's fashionable women sold kisses for $77 each. An Opera House lottery got off to a disastrous start when one of the winners came home to find that his son had been kidnapped.

On October 20, 1973, 16 years after building began, the Sydney Opera House was opened by Queen Elizabeth II of England. Since then it has hosted hundreds of concerts, operas, plays, exhibitions, and conferences each year. Demand for the building's halls is so great that bookings must be made up to a decade in advance. Visitors to the Opera House all agree that it possesses a unique and timeless beauty. It is, in the words of its designer, "a sculpture…a living thing."

Nobel prizewinner
Patrick White wrote
many novels, short
stories, plays, and
poems. Though his
novels are all set in
Australia, he shows a
wider vision embracing
universal themes.

LITERATURE

The Outback and the exploits of its inhabitants have always been a favorite subject of Australian writers and poets. Henry Lawson was the author of a number of well-loved bush stories including *The Loaded Dog*, a tongue-in-cheek tale of a faithful retriever that tries to return to its owner an explosive with its fuse burning much to the owner's horror! Lawson had a deep love for the Australian bush—"the nurse and tutor of eccentric minds, the home of the weird, and of much that is different from things in other lands."

Contemporary playwrights and authors have focused more on the attitudes and beliefs of Australians. In *The Tree of Man* (1955), Nobel prizewinning novelist Patrick White ridiculed many of the qualities that Australians admire about themselves. Understandably, the book sparked long and heated arguments among Australians.

The country also has a long tradition of children's literature. Prominent children's writers are Ivan Southall, Patricia Wrightson, Colin Thiele, and David Martin.

Aboriginal literature is also being compiled—recording traditional stories in books and other written forms. Aboriginal authors and poets have emerged as a strong creative force.

WALTZING MATILDA: THE UNOFFICIAL ANTHEM

It is an embarrassment to the nation that most Australians do not know the words of the national anthem, *Advance Australia Fair*. But this certainly cannot be said for *Waltzing Matilda*, a poem about an Outback wanderer (a swagman) who has a run-in with the law. This simple song, known to all Australians young and old, has been suggested as a replacement to the present national anthem.

Once a jolly swagman
   camped by a billabong,
Under the shade of a
   coolabah tree,
And he sang as he watched and
   waited till his billy boiled,
"Who'll come a-waltzing
   Matilda with me?"

Chorus
"Waltzing Matilda, waltzing
   Matilda,
"Who'll come a-waltzing
   Matilda with me?"
And he sang as he watched and
   waited till his billy boiled,
"Who'll come a-waltzing
   Matilda with me?"

Down came a jumbuck to
   drink at the billabong,
Up jumped the swagman and
   grabbed him with glee,

And he sang as he shoved that
   jumbuck in his tuckerbag,
"You'll come a-waltzing Matilda
   with me."

Up rode the squatter mounted
   on his thoroughbred,
Down came the troopers, one,
   two, three,
"Where's that jolly jumbuck you've
   got in your tuckerbag?
You'll come a-waltzing Matilda
   with me."

Up jumped the swagman and
   jumped into that billabong,
"You'll never take me alive,"
   said he.
And his ghost may be heard
   as you pass by that billabong:
"Who'll come a-waltzing
   Matilda with me?"

billabong: sheltered waterhole
billy: water can
Matilda: bed roll

jumbuck: sheep
tuckerbag: food bag
squatter: farmer

FILMS

Mel Gibson has estab-
lished himself as a
serious actor with
versatile talents.

Australia was a leading producer of movies during the era of silent films, holding the distinction of creating the world's first full-length feature film, *Soldiers of the Cross*. Nevertheless, after a promising start in 1896, the young local industry was soon overwhelmed by overseas productions, particularly from Hollywood. The Australian film industry virtually disappeared halfway through this century because of American control of the local film distribution networks.

Going to the movies, however, remains a very popular pastime with Australians. Theaters come in all shapes and sizes, ranging from city complexes seating hundreds in air-conditioned comfort to the makeshift theater in the local townhall or the club auditorium of small towns.

The film industry has experienced a revival in the past two decades, drawing extensively upon the work of local writers for their scripts.

Australian movies have experienced a strong resurgence in popularity, both locally and overseas. Leading the charge was the *Mad Max* series starring Mel Gibson. When the first *Mad Max* movie was released in the United States, it attracted quite a cult following. The third and last movie in the series, *Mad Max: Beyond Thunderdome,* was a Hollywood-style production co-starring rock star Tina Turner.

Wider international recognition came with the release of *Crocodile Dundee* and its sequel, which earned its producer and star, Paul Hogan, hundreds of millions of dollars overseas. The movie grossed top dollar among local audiences, who were greatly amused by its unrealistic portrayal of Australia. Hogan, who previously worked as a rigger on the Sydney Harbor Bridge, has since been lured to Hollywood along with a number of other famous figures in the local movie industry such as actors Mel Gibson and Nicole Kidman, and director Peter Weir.

Paul Hogan's big break came when he produced and starred in *Crocodile Dundee*, an adventure comedy about the stereotypical Australian.

JUST DESSERTS

Australian audiences are well-known for their appreciation of performing artists. One artist in particular, the prima ballerina Anna Matveena Pavlova, captured the hearts of the public during her tour of Australia in the 1930s. In tribute to the young dancer, a local chef created a dessert consisting of a shell of meringue filled with whipped cream and fruit. The pavlova, as it became known, was an instant success and soon became a national dish. Two sopranos—Dame Nellie Melba and Dame Joan Sutherland—have also enjoyed the distinction of having desserts named after them.

LEISURE

AUSTRALIANS SPEND their free hours outdoors, enjoying the country's wide open spaces and pleasant weather. On weekends and holidays, people can be seen walking in the bush, relaxing at the beach or simply outdoors, enjoying the sunshine.

OUTDOOR LIVING

Australia's 74 million acres of protected forests are frequented by hikers, campers, and fishermen. Fly fishermen frequent secluded streams in search of elusive Brown trout and Rainbow trout. Those after larger catches can try their hand at offshore fishing, with the prospect of hooking shark, marlin, or tuna.

Parks and plazas are common locations for open-air rock concerts, plays and community celebrations, and restaurants and hotels have outdoor sections for guests who wish to sample the night air.

VACATIONS

Australians are great travelers, in their own country and overseas. Going away and working overseas for a couple of years is considered part of the growing-up process. The most popular destinations for Australians going abroad are Europe and Great Britain. In addition, many also save up for package tours of Asian countries and islands in the Pacific.

Australians like to spend a lot of time outdoors and are spoiled by the choice of activities available. The impressive landscape and magnificent weather (*opposite and above*) make sightseeing, bush-walking, and camping a real pleasure.

BEACH CULTURE

Australia boasts some of the best beaches in the world, with warm golden sands and turquoise-blue waters. Many of them are located in or within a reasonable distance of the capital cities. Sydney's Bondi Beach (pronounced "bohn-dai") is just 20 minutes from the city center. As the closest surfing beach to town, it attracts numerous board riders as soon as the first rays of sunlight appear. Surfers Paradise, on Queensland's heavily developed Gold Coast, is another popular spot for local residents and tourists. The islands on the Great Barrier Reef and several others off central and north Queensland are excellent for beach vacations and for exploring the reef.

Australians have a passion for surfing, and Surfers Paradise on the Gold Coast attracts thousands of surfers each day.

CRICKET

Cricket, Australia's only truly national sport, is played by millions of sportsmen each season in their backyards, open fields, and sporting ovals (a flat stretch of land for sports). Similar to baseball, it is played by two teams of 11 men, each side taking turns to bat and bowl. The fielding side's pitcher, known as the bowler, hurls a small, hard ball in a round, overarm action at three waist-high wickets the 22 yard-length of the hard turf, called a pitch. The wickets, or stumps, are protected by a batsman from the opposing team, who attempts to strike the ball with a willow bat. A successful hit may lead to the opportunity of scoring runs, which involves the batsman and a partner running to opposite ends of the pitch.

The batsman is out if the ball strikes the stumps or hits the batsman's body on the way to the stumps. Batsmen are also dismissed if the ball is caught after being hit by the batsman or if the stumps are struck while the batsman is running between the stumps. The side that scores the most runs before being all dismissed (bowled out) wins the game.

Cricket is the most popular sport in Australia, both with players and spectators. Test matches and one-day internationals can attract crowds of 80,000.

The traditional form of cricket is known as a test match and is played over five days, each side getting the opportunity to bat twice. Even then, the match may end in a draw. A recent variation of the test match, the one-day match, is a shorter but more dynamic form of the game. It is often played at night under strong spotlights. Both test matches and one-day games attract huge, enthusiastic crowds, who turn out each summer to follow the fortunes of national cricketers against teams from the West Indies, Pakistan, India, Sri Lanka, New Zealand, and England. The regular test matches against England are of special significance, since both teams fight for The Ashes, an urn containing the ashes of a wicket symbolizing the death of England's previous dominance of cricket. The urn and its contents were first presented to Australia at the end of the last century, following England's defeat by a touring Australian team.

THE LEGEND OF THE DON

Regarded at the peak of his career as the perfect Australian, the country's greatest sporting hero is today a living legend. Sir Donald Bradman, known simply as the Don, first brought his uncanny talent with the cricket bat to national attention as a youth when he scored a century (more than one hundred runs) in an inter-state match in 1927. After being included in the national team, the Don went on to score numerous centuries, double centuries, and triple centuries—breaking countless long-standing records along the way. Under his captainship in the 1930s and 1940s, the Australian cricket team was invincible. Bradman himself retired in 1948 with a test-batting average of 99.9 runs, a record that has never since been matched

The Don was also at the center of a bitter dispute that almost resulted in the breaking off of friendly relations between Australia and England. In a desperate effort to defeat the world's greatest batsman, the captain of the English cricket team that toured Australia at the end of 1933 resorted to unusual and highly dangerous tactics. Using the tactics known as bodyline, the English bowlers were instructed to bowl their balls not at the stumps, but at the batsman's body instead. Although bodyline tactics proved to be immediately successful even against the Don, the terrible injuries suffered by the Australian batsmen caused widespread public outrage against England. Cricket, a game steeped in the venerable traditions of sportsmanship and fair play, had become a bitter war. England won the Test series, but English cricket lost the respect and admiration of the Australian people. Bodyline tactics were declared illegal the following year.

Australia has produced a regular stream of world-class tennis players.

SUMMER SPORTS

TENNIS While cricket is undoubtedly the most popular spectator sport in Australia, its claim to being the sport most Australians like to play is being threatened by tennis. More than half a million Australians play tennis at an organized, competitive level, maintaining a sporting dominance that has produced a number of international tennis superstars, including Grand Slam winner and four-time Wimbledon champion Rod Laver, and Wimbledon champions Pat Cash, Evonne Cawley, and John Newcombe. Australia's national tennis teams have won the Davis Cup a total of 19 times since 1950. The Australian Open, held in the state of Victoria, is one of the four Grand Slam events of international tennis and attracts the world's top tennis players.

GOLF Although golf is played all year round in Australia, the major tournaments are held only during summer. Australia is a favorite destination for avid overseas golfers who come on special golfing vacations. There are numerous clubs with world standard courses that are uncrowded and charge modest fees. Four figure annual membership fees, common in the United States and Japan, are unheard of in Australia, even at the country's most exclusive golf courses. Australia's current top golfer is Greg Norman, known as the "Great White Shark." A hard driver of the ball and accurate putter on the green, Norman spent his youth on the Queensland coast where he spent his days surfing and caddying at a local club. Each year, Australia plays host to one of international golfing's major tournaments, the Australian Open.

Golfing in Australia is not the rich person's sport it tends to be in other countries. The clubs have well-maintained courses and charge reasonable fees.

WINTER SPORTS

FOOTBALL The sports calendar in the winter months is dominated by Australia's four types of football: Rugby Union, Rugby League, Australian Rules, and soccer. All four variations of football can be likened to a less structured and more free-flowing version of American gridiron football. Unlike American players, Australian football players do not wear any protective clothing and must rely on their fitness, wits, and an element of luck to escape serious injury during the season.

The oldest code, Rugby Union, is run on an amateur basis. Many of its players opt for a professional career in Rugby League, which closely resembles Union. League has a strong following in the states of Queensland and New South Wales. Australia is one of the world's top-ranking teams in Rugby Union, and became the world champion side in 1991 by beating England in the World Cup final. By far the most popular code is Australian Rules, a national sport originating in the state of Victoria. Similar to Gaelic football, it is played on an enormous oval field; games are hard and fast, with the action shifting from one team's end to the other in the space of seconds. Australian Rules matches can draw huge crowds of enthusiastic fans. One grand final was attended by over 110,000 spectators, 1% of the nation's population at the time.

Australia's growing European ethnic population and increasing concerns over the safety of the football codes has resulted in soccer's emergence as one of the country's largest participant sports. In addition to school and club teams, Australia has a national soccer team that competes in the World Cup. They are called the Socceroos, and the highpoint in Australian soccer came in 1974 when they qualified for the World Cup finals in Germany. Competitive soccer is played at club level and Australia has had a National Soccer League since 1977.

HAVING A PUNT

At 2:40 p.m. on the first Tuesday in November each year, workers put down their tools and supervisors interrupt inspections. Across the country, ears and eyes are glued to radios and television sets to witness the running of the premier event in the national horse-racing calendar: The Melbourne Cup. Although all Australians indulge in a bet (a punt) on the outcome of the two-mile event, Cup winners are very hard to pick, and luck plays as much a hand as knowledge. This race has become an international thoroughbred classic and no other has such a strong hold on the Australian public.

Australians love betting on the outcome of any race. One of the more unusual races is the camel race.

Australians are avid race-goers and meets are held all over the country in the large city courses such as Flemington and Randwick, and in numerous local courses of smaller towns. In addition to horse racing, Australians turn out to see harness racing and greyhound races.

The Australians' love of racing also extends to motor vehicles. In addition to the annual Tooheys 1,000, an endurance race dominated by locally-made cars, the country hosts American-style NASCAR races and a European-based Group A production car race series. In November each year, Adelaide, state capital of South Australia, is the scene for the final race in the international Formula One Grand Prix competition. Like the famous Monaco circuit, the Adelaide Grand Prix is held through the city's streets, giving residents the chance of seeing cars whiz by at speeds over 180 mph. Famous Australian Formula One world champions are Jack Brabham and Alan Jones.

OUTBACK LEISURE ACTIVITIES

Although Australians like to identify themselves with the country or the Outback, there are very few true "bushies" left. Lots of the old farms have given way to huge stations (ranches) with beautiful "homesteads" and a comfortable lifestyle. Outback people tend to lead very busy lives. Weekdays are filled with farmwork and housework, but weekends can include tennis parties and leisure activities associated with the country. For women of the Outback, the local branch of the Country Women's Association (CWA) provides welcome relief from household chores. The CWA has a wide range of activities that may include arts and crafts, cooking, or in-depth study of a particular country or current affairs. Young people look forward to social activities like "woolshed" dances or the very formal B&S (Bachelor and Spinster) Balls.

Outback families like to get together on weekends for a picnic or a barbecue.

Outback people are very friendly and play host to people visiting the area, providing warm hospitality. The men wear broad-brimmed hats to keep the strong sun out, work long hours from sunrise to sunset, and speak with a broad Australian accent. They love telling each other and their visitors tall or exaggerated stories about life in the Outback. The "Great Yarns" often concern their sheep or cattle dogs called the "kelpie," or the dreadful plague of flies called the "blowies."

FESTIVALS

AUSTRALIANS CELEBRATE eight national holidays a year. In addition, each state has its own holidays held at various times of the year. The two most important festivals in Australia are the two most significant celebrations of the Christian calendar: Easter and Christmas.

CHRISTMAS

Christmas festivities begin more than a month in advance, in November, with schools and church groups staging Nativity plays celebrating the birth of

Christ. They also organize nightly gatherings in parks to sing Christmas carols by candlelight. Special services are held in churches across the country on Christmas Eve.

Christmas Day is celebrated at home with the family and close friends. The highlight of the day is Christmas lunch, an extravagant affair that requires many weeks of preparation. It traditionally consists of roast turkey and ham, followed by pudding, which is doused in brandy and flamed before being served. Because Christmas falls in the middle of Australia's hot summer, many families instead prefer to hold a barbecue in the back garden or have a meal of cold meats and salads. The afternoon is the time for a nap to recover from the elaborate lunch or a light-hearted game of cricket with the kids.

Opposite: **Australia Day celebrations culminate in a spectacular display of fireworks above the city.**

Above: **Christmas at Bondi Beach, with an ingeniously-decorated Christmas tree.**

Above: **Australians feel most patriotic on Australia Day when they come out to watch re-enactments of the colonist's first landing in Sydney.**

Opposite: **The Anzac War Memorial in Melbourne is one of the monuments erected in remembrance of those who laid down their lives for their country.**

NATIONAL DAYS

AUSTRALIA DAY Also known as Foundation Day, Australia Day marks the anniversary of the arrival of the first British colonists (both free settlers and convicts) in Sydney Cove on January 26, 1788. The nation's birth is celebrated on this day rather than on Federation Day, the anniversary of the creation of the Federation of Australia in 1901. This is partly due to the inopportune date chosen for federation—January 1—a day traditionally reserved to recover from the excesses of New Year's Eve! Australia Day is celebrated throughout the country in open-air festivals in which people gather to watch re-enactments of the first landing and to take part in contests that pay tribute to the nation's culture and history. At night, fireworks light up the dusky skies high above the cities. Patriotic fervor is at its highest on Australia Day.

ANZAC DAY Each year, Australians honor those killed in war on Anzac Day, April 25. This particular date is the anniversary of the start of Australia's most disastrous military battle—the Gallipoli campaign of World War I in which the forces of the Australian and New Zealand troops (Anzacs) suffered horrendous casualties due to the poor preparation and leadership of their British commanders. Ironically, the man who masterminded the Gallipoli campaign was none other than Sir Winston Churchill, Britain's prime minister during World War II.

OFFICIAL HOLIDAYS

January 1	New Year's Day
January 26	Australia Day
March/April	Good Friday
	Easter Monday
April 25	Anzac Day
Early June	Queen's Birthday
December 25	Christmas Day
December 26	Boxing Day

Above: **War veterans parade down the streets to commemorate Anzac Day.**

Below: **Queen Elizabeth II's birthday is celebrated by a national holiday.**

Military services are held at dawn on Anzac Day at various war memorials during which a minute's silence is observed in tribute to those who died in battle. The service ends with the words "Lest we forget"—a reminder of the horrors of war and the contribution of those Australians who braved it to defend their nation. The service is followed by a parade of servicemen from the various wars Australia has engaged in. A special place of honor is reserved at the head of the march for the original Anzacs who took part in the Gallipoli campaign.

THE QUEEN'S BIRTHDAY The birthday of Queen Elizabeth II, queen of England and the Commonwealth, is celebrated every year on the second Monday of June in all states except Western Australia, where it is celebrated in October. In her role as the ceremonial head of state, the Queen each year delivers a special birthday speech.

AGRICULTURAL SHOWS

The annual agricultural show has now become a tradition of rural Australian life, although most shows take place in cities. The tradition was brought to Australia from Britain by the first settlers.

The agricultural show gives farmers the opportunity to show off their produce and catch up on the latest developments in agriculture. In addition to the judging of livestock and crops, awards are given for homemade arts and crafts, and a number of exhibitions are staged, including demonstrations by expert shearers (known as "gun shearers") and cattle roundup competitions. Their activities are accompanied by circus rides and games. For women and children of the bush, it is a wonderful opportunity to have some fun and to meet new people.

The Royal Easter Show is the biggest agricultural event in Australia. It attracts large numbers of exhibitors as well as crowds of buyers.

Most agricultural shows are held in late summer or autumn, and most towns host one show a year. The largest show held in Australia is Sydney's Royal Easter Show. Running for one whole week in early April, the show attracts millions of visitors each year who come to examine samples of the best farming produce in the nation and enjoy the show jumping and rodeo events. Although rodeos are a relatively new sport in Australia, several local riders figure among the top rodeo contestants in the United States.

Several wine festivals are held each year to let visitors sample the products of Australia's vineyards. Australian wine is now gaining recognition worldwide and exports are increasing.

More specialized agricultural shows include Ag-Quip, held each year in Gunnedah, a rural town in inland New South Wales. On display is an astonishing variety of farming equipment, including state-of-the-art machinery costing several million dollars for each piece of equipment. The show attracts many overseas buyers in search of sophisticated and efficient methods to boost their crop production.

Wine-producing areas host district festivals to display their wines. These festivals, lasting up to several weeks, include outdoor picnics, wine-making demonstrations, and tours of vineyards. Free wine is also available for tasting, but enthusiastic visitors are warned to leave their cars at home or risk punishment under Australia's strict drunk-driving laws!

ARTS FESTIVALS

Numerous arts festivals are held throughout the year in Australia's cities to encourage visits from overseas artists and to help develop local talent.

The best known arts festival is the Adelaide Festival of the Arts, held on even-numbered years. During the festival, local and overseas artists, performers, and musicians flock to South Australia's capital to take part in plays, concerts, streetside singing and dancing, and exhibitions.

Similar festivals are held in Melbourne (the Moomba Festival) and Sydney (Sydney Festival) each year. Moomba—an Aboriginal word that means "let's get together and have fun"—is a 30-year-old festival in the Mardi Gras spirit held during the first two weeks of March. There are more than 200 events, and everything culminates in a grand procession of floats. Highlights of the month-long Sydney Festival are free open-air performances by the Sydney Symphony Orchestra and the Australian Opera Company.

During the cities' week-long festivals, residents and visitors get to enjoy open-air concerts.

MUSIC FESTIVALS

Music festivals are also popular in Australia. At the beginning of each year in January, the town of Tamworth, New South Wales, hosts the Australian Country Music Festival. The festival was started in the early 1970s by a local radio deejay who referred to the town as "the country music capital of Australia." The 10-day festival attracts more than 30,000 visitors. Some of the music is authentic Australian, but many of the songs performed are influenced by American country music. Local country musicians, who enjoy a large following in Australia, compete for the coveted "golden guitar" awards given in recognition of excellence. A giant scale model of the award stands on the town's outskirts, welcoming visitors to the city.

One of the highlights of the year for Sydney's gay community is the annual Gay Mardi Gras. Sequins, feathers, and makeup are a must.

UNUSUAL FESTIVALS

Australians will give any excuse for a party, as evidenced by some of the more bizarre festivals held in the country. These include Darwin's Beer Can Regatta and the Camel Cup, a camel race held in Australia's Outback. During the Gay Mardi Gras, held in Sydney each year, the city's homosexual community takes to the streets in outrageous costumes. They and their elaborate floats are cheered on by thousands of onlookers as they make their way to an all-night party known as the Sleaze Ball.

110

THE BEER-CAN REGATTA

People take their beer drinking seriously in Darwin, in Australia's far north. In addition to being the chief city of the Northern Territory, the town is also known as the beer-drinking capital of the world since it is believed that Darwinians hold the distinction of consuming more beer per head than residents of any other place in the world. To keep up with the great demand, the town's breweries package their ales in the world's largest beer bottle: the half-gallon "Darwin stubbie."

Many of the drinkers in Darwin are in fact gathering the raw materials for a highly unusual race. Every June, Darwinians gather to cheer on participants in the premier event in their racing calendar: the Beer Can Regatta. Contestants take to the water in homemade boats, ranging from simple rafts to impressive model galleons, all made from thousands of empty beer cans. The race is the highlight of a day of festivities which, of course, includes much beer drinking. The citizens of Alice Springs, in the Northern Territory's south, also hold an annual boat race, known as the Henley-on-Todd Regatta (a humorous derivative from the British Henley-on-Thames Regatta). Undeterred by the fact that the Todd, the "river" on which the race is held, actually contains no water, the locals sail their boats on metal tracks. Later in the day, contestants return to the dry river bed to stage mock sea battles using bags of flour for ammunition.

FOOD

AUSTRALIA IS A COUNTRY of meat eaters: Australians eat more red meat per person than any other nation except New Zealand. This is hardly surprising considering that traditional Australian fare consists of meat for the three main meals of the day, with a breakfast of grilled lamb chops or beef steak, sausages, bacon and eggs; cold meats for lunch, and a dinner of roast or grilled lamb, beef, or pork. Meals are served with cooked vegetables and are accompanied by bread.

The influence of new cuisines and increasing health consciousness have blunted the Australian appetite for meat, although it remains the focus of most meals. Rising prices and the increasing pace of life have also affected the traditional Sunday roast, a sumptious lunch consisting of a roast joint of meat or a chicken that takes many hours to prepare.

Left: **Lamb is the favorite meat of Australian families. The usual Sunday lunch is roast lamb, potatoes, and two vegetables.**

Opposite: **The Big Pineapple in Queensland. Almost all the pineapples produced by Australia are grown in Queensland, and half are exported.**

FREE RANGE BEEF

Unlike their counterparts in the United States, Japan, and other countries, Australian diners prefer pasture-raised beef to grain-fed beef. Australians argue that cattle free to feed in pastures produce a more flavorful meat that is healthier because it contains less marbled fat.

Furthermore, many locals believe that the methods used to raise grain-fed cattle are cruel since the animals are not allowed to walk in the pastures and exercise. They also argue that these methods are wasteful since the cereals used to feed the cattle can instead be made into products for human consumption.

FOOD FOR THE OUTDOORS

A night out camping in the Australian bush is not complete without "damper" and "billy tea." Damper, an unleavened bread, is made from flour, salt, sugar, and milk. The ingredients are combined and cooked in the hot ashes of an open fire until a hard and blackened crust forms. When eaten with generous portions of golden syrup (treacle), it is known as "cocky's joy." The perfect drink to have with damper is billy tea. After boiling water in a camp can (known as a "billy"), a few tea leaves and the odd gum tree leaf are thrown in for about a minute. After allowing the leaves to settle by tapping the billy with a stick, the handle is firmly grasped and swung in a wide circle several times to cool down the tea. To avoid disaster, this last step should be left to those with experience!

Billy tea and damper: the prerequisites of life in the bush. Damper, or soda bread, was brought by early settlers who were reluctant to eat native products. Billy tea is boiled in a billy, a tin can with a lid.

The influence of immigrants from the Mediterranean has led to a widespread cafe society. Eating out of doors appeals to the informal and relaxed Australian character.

Fast foods, which cater to the typical Australian outdoor lifestyle, have grown in favor in the past few years.

The hamburger, made popular by American soldiers stationed in Australia during World War II, has become a local institution. Hamburgers sold at small neighborhood shops (known as "corner shops") are invariably huge, cramming a beef patty, bacon, a fried egg, cheese, onions, lettuce, tomatoes, beetroot, cucumber, and a slice of pineapple into a buttered bun. Eating such a hamburger is a studied art!

Equally popular with everyone is the meat pie, a fist-sized fast food that can be eaten on the run. Meat pies are now viewed as a typical Australian food.

BUSH TUCKER

The recent assault of foreign dishes on Australian palates has rekindled an interest in bush tucker as an alternative and easily-identifiable, distinctive Australian cuisine. Bush tucker focuses on edible animals and plants that are unique to Australia. Far from being a new culinary form, it has been practiced by the Aborigines for 40,000 years. During their long association with the country, Aborigines have exploited what would seem to be the most unlikely sources of food. These include the Witchetty grub, a fat, white slug-like creature that inhabits the bush of the same name, and which was eaten raw. Today, Witchetty grubs are exported internationally as "wood lobsters," with the recommendation to serve them lightly sauteed with a few herbs and spices.

Although the kangaroo formed a staple part of the Aboriginal diet, European settlers are generally less than enthusiastic about eating the country's national emblem. Nevertheless, kangaroo steaks, stews, and kangaroo tail soups were all a popular part of Australia's recent culinary past. Kangaroo tail soup was in fact so popular in the 1960s that it was canned for export. Crocodile steaks have met with a better reception. There is an undoubted secret satisfaction in eating crocodile, since each year one or two unfortunate swimmers fall victim to these beasts.

If a crocodile or kangaroo is not handy, hearty meals can be had from snakes, goannas (large omniverous lizards), turtles, birds, all kinds of fish and eels, ants, wild bees, wild cereals and grasses, and native roots, fruits and figs, as well as the resin from parasitic scale insects living on Mulga trees. Plants and smaller animals are generally eaten raw. Larger animals are traditionally roasted in hot coals.

In addition to its exotic appeal, bush tucker is nutritious and tasty. Those adventurous enough to give it a try no longer have to venture to Australia's Outback, but instead can visit a growing number of restaurants specializing in this unique cuisine.

FAVORITE DISHES

Some foods have become so popular with Australians that they are regarded as culinary institutions. They include:

PUMPKIN SCONES A long domestic tradition in northern Australia, pumpkin scones enjoyed a recent revival under the hands of former Federal Senator Flo' Bjelke-Petersen, who baked vast quantities of the little snacks to sustain her husband, then premier of Queensland, Joh Bjelke-Petersen, through the rigors of government. The scones obviously worked, since Joh Bjelke-Petersen enjoyed an unparalleled career in Australian politics, becoming by far the longest-serving state premier in the nation's history. He was also the most flamboyant and controversial premier in modern Australian politics.

An attack of nationalism has led some restaurants to serve dishes with names like rack of lamb Bendigo (roast lamb), Hobart shoulder (roast lamb), and Beaudesert lamb (roast lamb).

PUMPKIN SCONES

1 tablespoon butter	¼ cup milk
3 tablespoons sugar	¾ cup pumpkin (cooked and mashed)
1 egg (beaten)	2 cups self-rising flour
pinch of salt	

1. Cream butter with sugar until mixture is white and creamy.
2. Add beaten egg, milk, mashed pumpkin, sifted self-rising flour, and pinch of salt, and mix well.
3. Knead mixture into smooth dough.
4. Roll dough to about half an inch thick and cut small circles with scone-cutter.
5. Bake in hot oven for 15 to 20 minutes.

LAMINGTONS These delicate little sponge cakes are particularly popular at festivals and shows. Made from flour, eggs, milk, sugar, butter, and vanilla, the baked cake is sliced into two-inch cubes that are then dipped in chocolate. A sprinkle of coconut gives the lamington its delightful speckled look. The lamington is also connected to Queensland politics. It is said to have been created by the wife of 19th century Queensland governor, Baron Lamington, who served the cake bearing his name to his campaign workers.

The Jolly Jumbuck in a Tuckerbag is a more stylized variation of the favorite meat pie.

The pavlova, rich with whipped cream and ice-cream, is a wonderful dessert that should appeal to anyone with a sweet tooth.

PAVLOVA The Pavlova or "pav" is a favorite dessert created earlier this century by Western Australian chef Bert Sachse in honor of ballerina Anna Matveena Pavlova. The pavlova consists of a crisp, smooth shell of meringue, filled with whipped cream and fruit.

ANZAC BISCUITS First made during World War I by Australian mothers for their boys who were fighting overseas, Anzac biscuits are crisp and long lasting. They are also extremely hard and some can easily double as a tent peg hammer or a heavy-duty paper weight! Anzac biscuits have a pleasant gingery tang, and contain ginger, coconut, brown sugar, and golden syrup.

VEGEMITE A thick, black, yeast extract made by the Kraft Company, Vegemite is a long-time favorite stand-in for sandwich fillings and an ingredient in many savory dishes. Vegemite sandwiches are best made using thick slices of freshly-baked white bread. After generously buttering the slices, apply a small amount of Vegemite. Those unacquainted with its unique flavor should then proceed with caution, taking only modest bites and having a large drink on hand to wash it down. Definitely an acquired taste, the immense popularity of Vegemite among Australians is a frequent source of wonder to overseas visitors.

VEGETABLES AND FRUITS

Vegetables grown in Australia tend to be of a larger size than elsewhere in the world. Carrots can be more than 12 inches long. Tomatoes grow as big as grapefruit. One of the most popular vegetables is pumpkin, which can be cooked in all kind of dishes. Other popular vegetables are sweet potatoes, eggplants, cucumber, zucchini, lettuce, cabbage, beans, and peas. Bought in supermarkets or at open-air markets, vegetables are usually fresh and crisp.

Fruits are abundant and available all-year-round, since they can be grown in various parts of the country at different times. The usual ones are apples, pears, oranges, and peaches. Strawberries are at their best around Christmas, and are quite cheap, as are plums, cherries, bananas, pineapples, and grapes. Exotic fruits like avocados, mangoes, and papayas are also available, although they can be rather expensive.

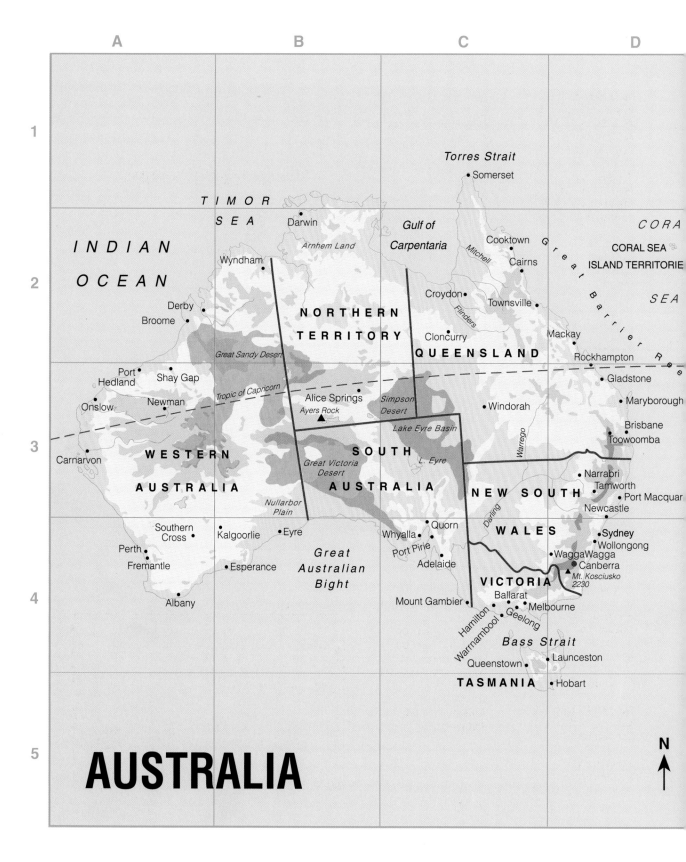

	A	B	C	D

1

Torres Strait
• Somerset

T I M O R

S E A

Darwin
•

C O R A

2

I N D I A N

Arnhem Land

Wyndham
•

Gulf of
Carpentaria

Cooktown
•

CORAL SEA

ISLAND TERRITORIE

O C E A N

Mitchell

Cairns
•

Great Barrier R

SEA

Derby
•
Broome
•

N O R T H E R N

Croydon
•

Townsville
•

T E R R I T O R Y

Flinders

Cloncurry
•

Mackay
•

Great Sandy Desert

Q U E E N S L A N D

Rockhampton
•

Port
Hedland
•
Shay Gap
•

Tropic of Capricorn

Alice Springs
•

*Simpson
Desert*

Gladstone
•

Onslow
•

Newman
•

Ayers Rock
▲

Lake Eyre Basin

Windorah
•

Maryborough
•

3

Carnarvon
•

W E S T E R N

S O U T H

L. Eyre

Warrego

Brisbane
•
Toowoomba
•

*Great Victoria
Desert*

A U S T R A L I A

A U S T R A L I A

N E W   S O U T H

Narrabri
•
Tamworth
•

Port Macquar
•

*Nullarbor
Plain*

W A L E S

Newcastle
•

Southern
Cross
•

Kalgoorlie
•

Eyre
•

Whyalla
•

Quorn
•

Darling

Sydney
•
Wollongong
•

Perth
•

Port Pirie
•

WaggaWagga
•
Canberra
•

Fremantle
•

Esperance
•

*Great
Australian
Bight*

Adelaide
•

V I C T O R I A

▲
*Mt. Kosciusko
2230*

4

Albany
•

Mount Gambier
•

Ballarat
•
Melbourne
•

Hamilton
•
Warrnambool
•
Geelong
•

Bass Strait

Launceston
•

Queenstown
•

T A S M A N I A

Hobart
•

5

AUSTRALIA

N
↑

Adelaide C4
Albany A4
Alice Springs B3
Arnhem Land B2
Ayers Rock B3

Ballarat C4
Bass Strait C4
Brisbane D3
Broome A2

Cairns C2
Canberra D4
Carnarvon A3
Cloncurry C2
Cooktown C2
Coral Sea Island
  Territories D2
Coral Sea D2
Croydon C2

Darling, river C4
Darwin B2
Derby A2

Esperance B4
Eyre B4

Flinders, river C2
Fremantle A4

Geelong C4
Gladstone D3
Great Australian Bight B4
Great Barrier Reef D2
Great Sandy Desert B2
Great Victoria Desert B3
Gulf of Carpentaria C2

Hamilton C4
Hobart D5

Indian Ocean A2

Kalgoorlie B4

Lake Eyre Basin C3
Lake Eyre C3
Launceston D4

Mackay D2
Maryborough D3

Melbourne C4
Mitchell, river C2
Mount Gambier C4
Mount Kosciusko D4

Narrabri D3
New South Wales C3
Newcastle D3
Newman A3
Northern Territory B2
Nullarbor Plain B3

Onslow A3

Perth A4
Port Hedland A3
Port Macquarie D3
Port Pirie C4

Queensland C2
Queenstown C4
Quorn C4

Rockhampton D2

Shay Gap A3
Simpson Desert C3
Somerset C1
South Australia B3
Southern Cross A4
Sydney D4

Tamworth D3
Tasmania C5
Timor Sea B1
Toowoomba D3
Torres Straits C1
Townsville C2
Tropic of Capricorn B3

Wagga Wagga D4
Warrego, river C3
Warrnambool C4
Western Australia A3
Whyalla C4
Windorah C3
Wollongong D4
Wyndham B2

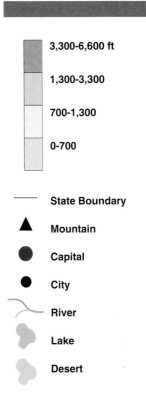

3,300-6,600 ft

1,300-3,300

700-1,300

0-700

— State Boundary

▲ Mountain

● Capital

● City

～ River

Lake

Desert

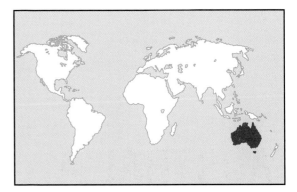

QUICK NOTES

AREA
2,967,909 square miles

POPULATION
17.5 million

NATIONAL FLOWER
Golden Wattle

STATES AND TERRITORIES
New South Wales, Queensland, Tasmania, Victoria, South Australia, Western Australia, Northern Territory, Australian Capital Territory, Jervis Bay Territory

NATIONAL CAPITAL
Canberra

STATE CAPITALS
Adelaide, Canberra, Sydney, Melbourne, Darwin, Hobart, Brisbane, Perth

GEOGRAPHICAL FEATURES
Ayers Rock (Uluru)
Great Dividing Range
Great Barrier Reef
Lake Eyre, a salt lake

HIGHEST POINT
Mt. Kosciusko (7,310 feet above sea level)

LOWEST POINT
Lake Eyre (53 feet below sea level)

MAJOR EXPORTS
Coal, minerals, ores, metals, meat, cereal, and textiles, including wool and cotton

CURRENCY
The Australian dollar, A$ ($1 = A$1.43)

MAJOR RELIGION
Christianity

NATIONAL LANGUAGE
English

IMPORTANT ANNIVERSARIES
Australia Day (January 26)
Anzac Day (April 25)

LEADERS IN POLITICS
Sir Edmund Barton (first prime minister, 1901–03)
Sir Robert Gordon Menzies (Liberal prime minister, 1939–41, 1949–66)
Gough Whitlam (Labor prime minister, 1972–75)
Robert James Lee Hawke (Labor prime minister, 1983–1991)
Paul Keating (Labor prime minister, 1991–present)

GLOSSARY

Aborigines	Earliest inhabitants of Australia.
billabong	Sheltered waterhole.
billy	Cylindrical container for liquids with a close-fitting lid.
bloke	Slang meaning man or guy.
bush	Countryside.
corroborees	Sacred Aboriginal ceremonies, in which dancers paint Dreamtime symbols on their bodies.
didgeridoo	An Aboriginal wind instrument consisting of a hollow pipe made from a tree log.
jumbuck	Sheep.
Koori	Name by which the Aborigines call themselves.
matilda	Bed roll, usually carried by swagmen.
nipper	A young child.
Outback	Remote, sparsely-populated country region.
over	The six throws taken by a bowler in a cricket match before changing ends or changing bowlers.
squatters	People who settled on land belonging to the state to run stock.
stations	Sheep farms.
swagman	Person who roams the Outback in search of work.
tinnie	A can, usually of beer.
transportation	A system of punishment whereby criminals and convicts, mainly from Britain and Ireland, were exiled to Australia.

BIBLIOGRAPHY

Australia in Pictures, Lerner Publishing Co., Minneapolis, Minn., 1990.

Horne, Donald: *The Story of the Australian People*, Reader's Digest, Sydney, Australia, 1985.

Kelly, Andrew: *Australia*, Bookwright Press, New York, 1989.

Lawson, Henry: *The Bush Undertaker and Other Stories*, Angus & Robertson, Sydney, Australia, 1970.

Luling, Virginia: *Aborigines*, Silver Burdett, Englewood Cliffs, NJ, 1979.

Stark, Al: *Australia: A Lucky Land*, Dillon, Minneapolis, Minn., 1987.

INDEX

INDEX

INDEX